BILLIE JEAN
KING

Tennis
to Win

with KIM CHAPIN
drawings by
Gerald McConnell

PUBLISHED BY POCKET BOOKS NEW YORK

TENNIS TO WIN

Harper & Row edition published 1970

POCKET BOOK edition published March, 1974

3rd printing..........................April, 1974

Ⱬ

This POCKET BOOK edition includes every word contained
in the original, higher-priced edition. It is printed from
brand-new plates made from completely reset, clear, easy-to-
read type. POCKET BOOK editions are published by POCKET
BOOKS, a division of Simon & Schuster, Inc., 630 Fifth
Avenue, New York, N.Y. 10020. Trademarks registered
in the United States and other countries.

Standard Book Number: 671-78370-X.
Library of Congress Catalog Card Number: 70-95969.
Top cover photo by Jerry Cooke, ©, Time Inc.
Bottom cover photo by Ken Regan.
Printed in the U.S.A.

In memory of
Clyde Walker

Contents

Foreword | A Word About Billie Jean King

In October, 1964, Billie Jean Moffitt of Long Beach, California, age twenty, went to Australia to play the grass-court circuit. At the time, she was only a few courses away from a degree in social science at Los Angeles State College and was engaged to a law student from California, Larry King, who later became her husband. She was also considered one of the best women tennis players in the world. Her reputation had been firmly established two years earlier when, at the age of eighteen, she upset Margaret Smith, the defending champion, in the second round of the 1962 Wimbledon Championships. In 1963 Billie Jean (also known as "Jilly Bean") had reached the finals of Wimbledon. By 1964 she had been a member of four winning Wightman Cup teams and one Federation Cup team, and had twice been ranked number two in the United States. In short, she was very nearly the complete tennis player. But she wasn't yet the best, so she set out for Australia to become just that—number one—and she brashly announced her goal to anyone who asked. "I was terrified," she said. "It's bad enough when you silently think about becoming number one, but when you tell everybody you suddenly feel that perhaps you're not going to make it."

She spent three months under the tutelage of Mervyn Rose, a former Australian Davis Cup star turned coach. Rose not only changed her forehand completely but he gave her a new approach to the attacking game. Should you hit your volleys crosscourt or down the line? What are the important points of the game? At 30–all, do you ever serve to the forehand? Her stay in Australia became not only a test of physical endurance and technical craftsmanship, but something of a cerebral exercise as well. At night Billie Jean fell into bed exhausted. She jogged, sprinted, did fast volley exercises against Roy Emerson, spent six or seven hours daily on the court and was fast becoming a thinking player. The three-month crash course was the culmination of a learning process which had begun seven years before on the public courts of Long Beach under her first coach, Clyde Walker, and was later continued by all-time great Alice Marble of Tarzana, California, and Frank Brennan of Upper Saddle River, New Jersey. She learned not only *what* she was doing right and wrong on the court, an easy-enough task, but *why* certain things worked and others didn't, and that is not easy at all.

The results of her dedication were extremely gratifying. In 1965 she reached the finals of the United States Championships for the first time, losing to Margaret Smith 7–5, 8–6. It was clear she had the potential to be the world's best. She was again on a victorious Wightman Cup team and was co-ranked number one in the United States with Nancy Richey.

The next three years were all hers. In 1966 she won her first Wimbledon singles title, again playing on winning Wightman and Federation Cup teams, and was ranked number one in the United States and in the world. In 1967 she defended her Wimbledon title with ease, won her first United States crown, was again a member of the successful Wightman Cup team (for the seventh time), helped the United States hold the Federation Cup (for the third time), and was again ranked number one in the world. In 1968 she won her first Australian singles title, turned professional, and took the Wimbledon as well, becoming the first woman in fourteen years to win the Championships three years in a row. She lost in the final round of the first United States Open Championships at Forest Hills but was again named World's Number One. A knee injury, which necessitated two operations, one in 1968 and one in 1970, hampered her effectiveness through the 1970 season. But in 1971, fully recovered, she re-emerged as the leading player of the Virginia Slims women's professional circuit and became the first woman athlete in history to earn more than $100,000. That same year she won her first U.S. Open Championship title.

In the following season, if there was any question about her having regained her top standing, she again earned more than $100,000 and also the French, English, and U.S. Championships, three of the four big tournaments (along with the Australian) that make up the Grand Slam of tennis.

Not just a great singles star, she has won the Wimbledon doubles championship eight times with four different partners—Karen Hantze Susman (twice), Maria Bueno, Rosemary Casals (four times), and Betty Stove.

Billie Jean King is more than just a great champion. Her contributions to the game have seldom been equaled. She has been coach, friend, and inspiration to a dozen rising young stars, has worked endless hours with those who showed interest, talent, or both, and has freely given her time and energies to working with underprivileged youngsters in public park areas. Once, when she knew she was going to be in New York for two weeks, she wrote to the Parks Department to offer her services in teaching tennis and giving clinics at public parks. When she did not receive an answer she wrote again and then phoned. She was told—nicely—that the Parks Department could not afford her. "But I don't want any money," she replied. During her stay in New York she spent eight hours a day at areas such as Bedford-Stuyvesant, hitting overheads, teaching the kids how to hit ground strokes, and exchanging quips with them. ("Hey, lady, tell us again how you met the Queen." "Lady, do you really make $50,000 a year?") Her love of the game has not gone unappreciated: she won the Marlboro Award for her contributions to tennis over the years, and she was presented with the National Service Bowl for the help and inspiration she has given to so many players.

After nearly a decade at or near the top of the game and a lifetime of experimenting and learning, Billie Jean is more than able to pass her accumulated knowledge on to you, whether your personal goals are to reach the top of the international tennis ladder or just to play well enough to enjoy the sport with family and friends. Either way, this book is for you. Enjoy it.

Gladys M. Heldman, Publisher
World Tennis Magazine

1 | What Tennis Is All About

Everything you do of an athletic nature is as much an extension of your personality as it is a reflection of your particular physical strengths and weaknesses. And playing the game of tennis is no exception. If you are on the quiet side you're probably not going to have a flamboyant or especially gregarious game but rather one that is controlled and well ordered. If you are naturally outgoing and bubbly, you're probably going to wind up with a style that is flashy and fast-paced. When I started to play tennis I thought it was silly to wait until the ball hit the ground before I hit it back across the net, and my coach had to force me away from the net so I could learn the ground strokes. That's just the way I was, and still am, I guess—impatient and a little too eager to run before I walk—and over the last thirteen years this attitude has colored my whole approach to the game. As you learn to play tennis, it is important to take into account whether you have good reflexes or are a little slow getting off your mark, or whether you have a lot of strength or maybe are not as overpowering as many of the players you will be encountering. But it is equally important to know and understand your likes and dislikes and relate them to the game. If you have a rotten volley, it's silly to rush the net a lot; it's just as silly to stay on the base line if what you would really rather do is hit big, booming serves and daring, slashing volleys. What I am suggesting is that eventually you are going to have to decide for yourself what sort of game you want to play, and that your personality and physical abilities should be equally important in your decision. Keep that in mind as you read this book.

There is no one absolutely correct way to play tennis any more than there is one absolutely correct way to throw a football or a baseball. After all, Tom Seaver doesn't pitch the same way that Steve Carleton does, and Joe Namath doesn't quarterback the New York Jets the same way Bob Griese runs the Miami Dolphins. But they are all effective in their own, highly individual way.

If you have seen very much tennis played, you will have noticed that very few players have the same overall approach to the game, regardless of their level. Some like to play the big serve-and-volley game, which is what I prefer, but others like to stay on the base line and hit ground strokes all afternoon. Many find a happy middle ground somewhere between these two extremes. Pancho Segura hits a two-handed forehand. Beverly Baker Fleitz doesn't hit any backhand at all; she is totally ambidextrous and hits both a right-handed and a left-handed forehand. Nancy Richey learned to play on slow, hard courts. She doesn't like to rush the net often, but compensates by hitting hard and accurate ground strokes from almost anywhere on the court. Margaret Smith Court uses her height and tremendous reach to simply overwhelm her opponents. And so it goes. Every player is a highly individual combination of his strengths and weaknesses.

The problem with youngsters watching one of these players is that they think: "Gee whiz. Margaret really rushes the net well. That's exactly what I should be doing." Or: "Nancy really likes to stay in the backcourt. That's where I ought to be." Well, that may or may not be true, but it's likely that a youngster doesn't know *why* a player plays in a certain way. That is what is important, and that is the sort of thing you eventually are going to have to work out for yourself.

Just as there is no one way to play tennis correctly, it follows that there is no one correct way to learn the game. Everyone has his own ideas. Should you put the biggest emphasis on power or on accuracy? Should you learn the volley before you learn the ground strokes? Is it better to practice by hitting a lot of balls and working on your strokes or by playing actual games and sets to get used to the pressures and strategies of match play? Naturally I have my own ideas about all of these things, and many more. But I won't presume to suggest that everything I'm going to talk about in the succeeding chapters is right for you personally. When I've lost a match, somebody always tries to tell me what I did wrong. Although I might listen to him, I then have to filter out what I don't think is relevant and consider only the advice I think sounds right for my game. You should find one person you feel really knows tennis and rely primarily on his or her advice. But at the same time you have to be receptive to new ideas. As you progress it won't take you long to find out what kind of forehand you want to hit, what sort of strategies you want to employ in a match, or even how seriously you want to play the game. But whatever your particular goal is, there are certain basic things you should know. To go back to baseball for a minute, Tom Seaver may throw that little ball differently from the way Steve Carleton does it, but they both get it over the plate with pretty good success. Until you become fully aware of your own strengths and limitations and can figure out for yourself *why* you want to do certain things, let me tell you the *hows,* and at the same time provide a basic frame of reference for what in the end will have to be your own personal decisions.

And do yourself another favor. After a few weeks, seek some more advice from other sources, either from other instructional books or from good players you may know personally. Then you'll have a good cross section of opinion to choose from and you'll be better able to sort out what's best for you.

For those of you who belong to the sports world's most neglected minority group—the left-handers—all I can say is that I'm right-handed and that this book is written from a right-hander's point of view. But don't be dismayed. Unlike golf, where it is a distinct handicap to be a lefty, or baseball, where it doesn't make much difference, tennis is a game in which it is a decided advantage to be left-handed. The balls you hit will have a spin the exact opposite of that to which your opponents are accustomed. In general, your opponents must reverse their normal thinking on match strategy 180 degrees, and presuming everything else is equal, you will have a real edge on them every time you step on the court. Besides, nearly everything I will talk about applies equally to right-handers or left-handers, and I don't believe you'll find much of a problem if you think "left" when I write "right," and vice versa.

Now, before I begin in earnest, I would like to make three points which should always be kept in mind while reading the rest of this book. First of all, tennis is not an easy game to learn. In fact, it is one of the most difficult. I have heard this not only from other good tennis players, but from athletes who have taken up the game as a second sport. Unless you happen to be extremely gifted, which most of us aren't, there is no such thing as instant gratification. Most of us can tee up a golf ball and hit it with a club, maybe not very far or very straight, but at least with some immediate, tangible result. Or most of us can take a bowling ball and after a few tries knock down a few pins. But hitting a moving object while you yourself are moving takes a pretty fair amount of coordination, and more yet is needed to hit it back across a net, thirty-six inches high at its lowest point, into a singles court that is thirty-nine feet long and twenty-seven feet wide. I've given clinics where it has taken some kids twenty minutes to hit just one ball across the net. For women it may be even tougher. Most women don't spend their childhood throwing a baseball or football around the back yard, and the resulting lack of development of this hand-to-eye coordination is another obstacle to overcome. I mention this not to discourage you, of course, but on the contrary, to make sure that you aren't discouraged when you can't dash crosscourt and hit a beautiful running backhand with grace and power the first few times you try. Tournament-level tennis requires speed, strength, stamina, skill, and a good bit of coordination, all of which can be developed. But not overnight.

In fact, I strongly believe this is why the game is so
satisfying to the more than nine million people who
play it in this country. Once you've learned to hit that
little fuzzy ball well, you know you've accomplished
something of which you can feel very proud. But there
is no such thing as the perfect tennis player, and that,
really, is half the enjoyment. I've won a lot of important
tournaments, and I can honestly say that even now I'm
not satisfied with the way I play. And no matter how
good you eventually become, you will always know that
there is a way to play just a little bit better. This is what
keeps you going and arouses your interest every time
you step on the court.

Another point. Thoreau first said, "Simplify, simplify," and although he probably didn't know too much
about tennis, that is exactly what he could have been
talking about. I'll be mentioning specific cases later on,
but in general try to remember that the act of striking
a tennis ball is the collective result of a series of essentially simple motions. The problems arise when players
—especially young ones but also a few who should
know better—add little frills to their stroke. In a few
cases there may be a specific reason for a kookie wind-
up, an extra-long backswing, or whatever, but most
of the time things like that are just extraneous equipment which should be discarded as soon as possible.

Usually this simplification process happens involun-
tarily after a player has solidified his game to the point
where he has no major weaknesses. Then, like the layers
of an onion, the excess baggage slowly is peeled off
until what is left is nothing more than—well, nothing
more than the basic shot itself. Why not, then, hit your
shots like this from the very beginning? And besides,

there is a more practical reason. The more economical your stroke, the less effort you expend and the less tired you will become, an increasingly important factor as you grow older. The most beautiful example of this economy in tennis today, I think, is Ken Rosewall. There is absolutely no wasted motion whatever in any of his shots. Everything he does is directly related to hitting the ball. If it isn't he simply doesn't do it.

The third point is also simply stated: Be bold. Even when you're starting out, you should hit the ball aggressively and with confidence. Accuracy is important, of course, and I'm not suggesting that you should be slugging balls over fences while all around you other players are hitting theirs politely in. But many men and most women, especially club players, play a soft, backcourt game characterized by a lot of lazy backcourt rallies. The main objective of most club players, of course, is to get enjoyment from the game, and they don't really care whether they're big winners as long as they have a lot of fun. Which is fine. However, for the young players who have competitive aspirations, who want to be somebody, I'm talking about another level of play entirely. Most of this comes back to personality. Now, I don't play what is considered a typical "woman's" game anyway. I play a fairly modern, aggressive, serve-and-volley game with very quick points. And it's not that difficult for men or women, older beginners or younger, to learn. A good tennis game is based in large measure on confidence, and confidence comes from hitting the ball as hard as you can and still keeping it in the court. The mistake so many young players make is in thinking that their *only* aim should be to keep the ball in play. They become so carried away with this idea that they spend all of their formative years on the base line trying to outlast their opponents. I never won a major junior tournament in my life, and I'm thankful for it. While a lot of the kids I grew up with were beating me when I was a young teen-ager, I was developing the type of aggressive, hard-hitting game that—once I learned to control it—allowed me to beat the skirts off them by the time I was nineteen or twenty. If you have any tennis ambitions at all, this is the approach to take. If you don't, eventually you're going to find that your opponents are going to take those soft, steady shots of yours and powder them right past you.

So these are the three things to keep in mind while you're learning to play tennis, or improving the game you already have: (1) It's not going to be easy. Have patience and don't expect miracles. (2) Simplify everything you do right down to the bare essentials. (3) Be bold. If you're going to make an error, make a doozy, and don't be afraid to hit the ball. It will help build the confidence you need to play your best tennis.

2 | The Ground Strokes

Despite modern-day emphasis on the so-called Big Game—a powerful service followed by a forcing first volley followed (if necessary) by a second and putaway volley—the ground strokes remain the fundamental shots of tennis, and consequently the most important. Taken together, the forehand and backhand, and their natural offspring, the return of service, provide the solid foundation upon which a sound tennis game is built. This becomes fairly obvious if you consider that during the course of a match you will hit more ground strokes —shots hit after the ball bounces on your side of the court—than all other shots combined. The return of service will be your first shot on half the points you play, and unless you plan to spend all of your time at the net, a game plan which no player yet has found practical to execute however much he may have wished to, the ground strokes are going to be the shots that determine whether you are an adequate tennis player or an erratic duffer. With only an average service you can still survive with a good forehand and backhand. On the other hand, if you have a booming serve but only so-so ground strokes, you will quickly find yourself helpless and frustrated against any opponent with a well-rounded game.

One preliminary note. Let me just say that the forehand and backhand should be taught, learned, and practiced together. There is nothing more annoying and unnecessary than for a player to take two or three extra steps just in order to avoid his backhand when that shot is just as easy to learn as a forehand, and in many respects easier. (Some players run around their forehands, but they're a rare breed.) What usually happens is that a beginner first learns the forehand drive, and once having reached the point where he can hit that shot fairly well, out of fear or distrust avoids the backhand like the plague. Don't ever make that mistake. I'm not dogmatic about very many things, but I am about this. If you spend a half hour on your forehand, spend a half hour on your backhand, and never, *never* run around either shot.

Partly because of tradition and partly because various court surfaces cause the ball to bounce differently, three classic grips have come into use over the years. I have often suspected this is merely to confuse beginners, because what most players wind up with, myself included, are grips that are not "classic" at all, although they may closely resemble one or two of them. The most important consideration is personal preference, and that is determined by nothing more sacred than comfort and feel. But to establish points of reference, let's first consider the three classic forehand grips.

To learn the Western forehand grip, place the racket on a flat surface, then grab hold of it and turn it so the face is perpendicular to the ground. The V formed by your thumb and first, or index, finger should then be pointed practically along the back side of the racket handle (the side away from the net). This is also the Western backhand grip, and both forehand and backhand are hit with the same side of the racket. This grip was popularized several decades ago by a group of California players, notably Maurice McLoughlin, but today it is considered outdated, awkward, and, like the carrier pigeon, something nice to know about but nothing you'll be likely to see.

The second forehand grip is the Eastern, which can be described in two ways: (1) take the Western grip and give the racket a quarter turn to the right (or conversely, turn your hand a quarter turn to the left); or (2) hold the racket perpendicular to the ground, put your right hand flush against the strings, then slowly bring your hand to the racket handle and take hold. When your fingers are spread comfortably, the V, again formed by your thumb and index finger, should be directly on top of the racket handle. This is the most popular forehand grip today, and nearly every player in recent years with an overpowering forehand has favored it.

The Continental forehand is acquired by turning the racket another eighth turn to the right so that the V now runs down the upper left corner of the handle. This is the grip learned by most Australians, but it requires more wrist control, and for a beginner it is an extremely difficult grip to be comfortable with.

I personally favor a grip about halfway between the classic Eastern and classic Continental, as shown in Figure 1, but I recommend strongly that you begin with the Eastern grip and stay with it until you have a fairly steady, consistent forehand. Then experiment a little bit and don't be intimidated by the "classics." If the grip that feels the best to you is somewhere near either the Eastern or the Continental, there won't be any serious problem. Regardless of what grip you use, however, under no circumstances should you choke the racket with a viselike or "club" grip. Remember, you are holding a tennis racket, not a suitcase. Hold the racket firmly enough so that it becomes a solid extension of your arm and won't be knocked loose when you hit a ball, but at the same time spread your fingers around the handle loosely enough so that you can "feel" the racket through all five fingers.

Also, you should grasp the racket as close to the butt of the handle as you can, within the bounds of comfort and control. Considering your shoulder as a fulcrum, every inch you can extend that racket will mean more power, as well as more reach. If this is simply too difficult at first, don't hesitate to choke up on the racket much in the same way a baseball hitter will choke up on his bat. However, this should be only a temporary measure, if for no other reason than when you choke up on the racket the butt will bang into your wrist and cause a loss of flexibility. As you gain strength and confidence, let the racket out further and further.

The backhand grip is essentially that of an exaggerated Continental forehand. To acquire it, hold the racket as though you were going to hit an Eastern forehand—with the V along the top of the racket—then twist the racket to the right (or your hand to your left) until you can comfortably lay your thumb along the back side of the handle (the side opposite the net, assuming you are facing the left sideline). You can posi-

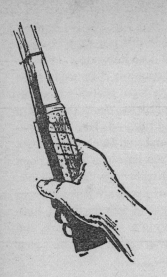

FIGURE 1
The Forehand Grip / My grip is about halfway between the classic Eastern and classic Continental. The V formed by my thumb and index finger is pointed along the upper-left corner of my racket, my fingers are spread comfortably, and the butt of the handle is even with the heel of my hand.

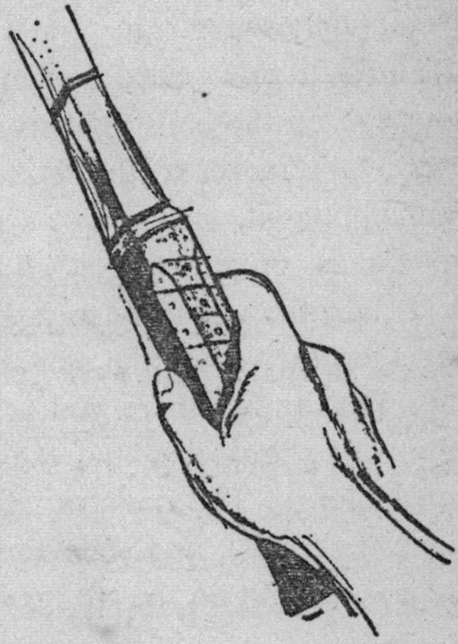

FIGURE 2
The Backhand Grip / This grip is essentially that of an exaggerated Continental forehand. The V has now shifted considerably to the left of where it was in Figure 1, and my thumb is wrapped firmly around the back side of the handle to give my shots maximum power and control.

tion that thumb in one of two ways. Either leave it right where it is, or move it so that it is wrapped more around the handle, as I have done in Figure 2. I recommend the second position because it is generally more comfortable and tends to give more control and power to your shots. For labeling purposes, this is the Eastern backhand grip, but the same rules—or lack of rules— apply here as apply to the forehand. Don't worry about names or labels, and once you have reached the point with this grip where your backhand is fairly reliable, experiment a little bit, and if necessary make changes so that you can hit the backhand with maximum comfort and feel. With this grip you're in the ballpark, and any small deviation from it won't in the least affect your ability to hit a good backhand.

Preparation is as important to the success of any tennis shot as the actual execution of the shot itself. After all, if you don't follow the ball well or move to it properly, it won't make too much difference what happens when you actually swing at it.

The first rule—need I even mention it?—is to keep your eye on the ball, right from the time it leaves your opponent's racket to the time you hit it. Don't look at your opponent, or his racket, or someone you know in the stands, or anything at all but that little fuzzy ball. And fight the tendency to jerk your head up and look into the other court the split second before you hit the ball. You know where you are, you know where your opponent should be, and the dimensions of the court don't change. The only variable in the equation is the flight of the ball, and you should watch it until you can see it land right on the strings of your racket. This takes a lot of concentration, but it is the first requirement of a good tennis game.

Your ready position should be equidistant between the two sidelines and about three feet behind the base line. What I will be expounding throughout this book is an aggressive, forceful approach to tennis, and you simply can't attack off your forehand or backhand if you are mired five to ten feet behind the base line.

The head of the racket should be held about waist high and pointed directly in front of you. It should not be pointed to your right or to your left, nor aimed at the sky or the ground, but directly in front of you. Nor should you be leaning to one side or the other. Your weight should be equally distributed on both legs and you should be on the balls of your feet—everybody says "Get on your toes," but that's impossible—and you should be ready to go to either your right or your left.

Once you see to which side of you the ball is coming, start moving toward it immediately, and by "toward it" I mean *forward*. A common fault of beginners is to run sideways and backward when they move after a ball. This should be discouraged at all costs. At the very least run directly parallel to the net, and at best run parallel to and in toward the net. There will, of course, be times when a ball will come in so deep that you'll have to move back in order to avoid hitting it off your shoetops. But, most of the time, unless your opponent has hit a really devastating shot, you'll have plenty of time to come in and it will be easier for you to hit an aggressive, attacking ground stroke. Learn this early. Bad habits are hard to break, and if you play tennis at all seriously, the habit of running backward all the time is one that is going to have to be broken sooner or later. Better sooner.

But whether you move forward or back, learn to hit the ball on the rise, or at least at the peak of its bounce. Every ground stroke should be hit waist high, the level of maximum power and control, and moving quickly to where you can hit the ball on the rise almost guarantees that this is what you will do. Just thinking about it will force you to get into position more rapidly. And the less time your opponent has to prepare for your return, the better off you'll be.

Of course, your opponent is not always going to co-operate and hit balls that bounce to the level you most prefer, and in order to hit everything waist high you're going to have to bend a lot. Bend from your knees, not your waist. For some reason most players, especially girls, have difficulty doing this and bend mostly from the waist—if indeed they bend at all—and lose most of their power and much of their balance. You obviously can't keep your back completely rigid, but your knees should be the primary elevators. If the ball bounces high, extend those legs and get up on the balls of your feet; if it bounces low, get down, as low as is necessary.

The Forehand

The forehand drive is best explained by breaking it down into its four main components: the early back-swing, the maximum backswing, the moment of contact, and the follow-through, as shown in Figures 3A through 3D. But as you learn the shot step by step, remember that in fact it is one continuous, unbroken motion. You should remain aware of the whole swing even as you consider each of its four phases. A consistent rhythm is extremely important to the success of the forehand (and, for that matter, all other shots), and a hitch anywhere along the line can only detract from its overall effectiveness.

In Figure 3A, I've just begun my backswing. I said earlier that in the ready position the racket should be approximately waist high. It should remain waist high right up until the time you actually hit the ball; no high or low backswing, but just a nice, easy, *level* swing. My right elbow is tucked lightly into my side, and my body is starting to coil up.

This is what I mean by "coil up." A cardinal rule in tennis has been to keep your body sideways to the net. Basically this is true, but the general interpretation is that your feet as well as your shoulders should be lined up so that they form a plane perpendicular to the net, and on the forehand side this presents all sorts of problems. If you hit a forehand with your feet lined up perfectly even and perfectly parallel to the net, your right forearm will come very close to hitting your left shoulder during the follow-through. This is extremely awkward, so why not keep your body out of the way of your swing right from the beginning. Take another look at Figure 3A. My feet are planted in such a way that a line connecting them will form approximately a forty-five-degree angle with the base line. This is what is known as an open stance. (In a closed stance I would be facing the right sideline head-on.)

Now, in Figure 3B, as my backswing reaches its maximum point, note that my shoulders are lined up

FIGURE 3
The Forehand/Note that my racket head remains approximately the same height off the ground until I hit the ball. I am swinging from a slightly open stance so that my body first coils during the backswing, then uncoils as I bring my racket forward to complete the shot.

C

D

perpendicular to the net even if my feet aren't. My torso
is, in effect, coiled up, and as I swing forward it will
uncoil and release all that wound-up power. At the
same time my shoulders will move out of the way of my
follow-through. If you do this properly you will feel
a slight tension in your back. Perfect.

In Figure 3B, also note that my racket head is still
waist high. My elbow, however, is no longer tucked
in against my body, but instead my arm is nearly fully
extended as though I were reaching for something to the
right of and slightly behind my right foot. The backswing—and the forward swing—is not so much circular
as it is linear. At the maximum point of your backswing your racket should be at no more than right angles
to the net. If you go back much further, you won't be
able to swing at the ball but will only be able to slap
at it.

What I have just described is a straight backswing.
In fact, most top players, myself included, add a slight
loop to this part of the swing to aid their rhythm and
timing. This is perfectly acceptable. Just don't exaggerate the loop too much. It does take more time, and
you don't want to have to rush your shots.

As you start the forward part of your swing, keep
your wrist firm, your arm steady, and your eye on the
ball, right up to the moment of contact. In Figure 3C,
I'm just hitting the ball. The head of my racket is even
with my wrist, or perhaps just a little bit ahead of it.
The racket is even with my left leg because that is the
point farthest along the swing where it is still parallel
to the net. Beyond that point the racket will begin to
circle around in front of me and I will begin to lose
power; before that point, I am still building up steam.

At the moment of contact my arm is still very nearly fully extended. Under no circumstances should you crowd the ball. This is a chronic problem, even for some players at the advanced level. They seem to feel more secure if they hit the ball when it's close to their body. But a tennis racket is twenty-seven inches long and your arm is another two and a half feet long, and the farther away from your body you hit the ball, the more power you're going to have. To make a baseball analogy, bending your arm and hitting the ball close to your side raises the same problems as those of a batter trying to hit an inside pitch. There's just no way to use maximum power.

During the forward part of the swing, a distinct weight shift will take place from your back foot (the right foot in the case of the forehand) to your front foot, as your racket is first drawn back and then brought forward. This is essential in order for you to get some of your body into the swing, but once you become aware of it, the weight transfer is so natural that it's not something you should worry about too much. Your concern is mainly whether you have established a firm, solid base so that you can maintain your balance throughout the entire shot. Keep your weight distributed on both of your feet, never one at a time, and think of your feet as the solid base of a pyramid to which the upper part of your body is attached. If you do this properly there will be no tendency to lurch forward or otherwise lose your balance, and the weight transfer from the back foot to the front will soon pretty much take care of itself.

Now, you're not going to notice this the first few hundred times you hit a tennis ball, but one day you're just going to know you've hit the perfect shot. You're going to know you've done everything just right—that you've moved into the ball properly, taken the correct backswing, and hit the ball dead even with your left leg—and when the ball lands on your strings with a solid *thunk* you'll be aware of a tingling sensation all through your body. That's what is known as "feel," and I know it sounds corny, but once you become aware of feel you've taken the first big step to becoming a good tennis player.

Obviously, feel is very subjective, but this particular feel is the result of two extremely tangible things. First, it means you have hit the ball dead in the pocket of your racket. The pocket, however, is not the center. The head of the racket is slightly egg-shaped, approximately twelve inches from top to bottom and nine inches from side to side. One inch below the center of that area is the pocket. That's where you get the most for your money, and that is where you should hit every shot. Second, if you hit the ball with a level, smooth, linear swing, at the moment of contact the ball actually compresses, the strings give slightly, and although you would need a stop-action picture sequence to show it, the ball stays on the strings for six to ten inches of the swing, then is catapulted out toward the other side of the net with power and control. These events, in combination, produce feel. As you swing, think about that pocket and remember what it feels like when the ball hits it.

After you hit the ball, there is a pronounced upswing during the follow-through, as shown in Figure 3D. In fact, during the follow-through I like to think "up and out," because what you actually want to do is lift the ball a little. The base line on the other side of the court is approximately seventy-eight feet away, and if you have made the proper level swing up to the moment of impact, it takes a definite lift and a lot of muscle to hit the ball beyond that line. But—avoid the common tendency to wrap the racket around your neck at the finish of the forehand. At the end my racket is pointed in the direction of the net and my arm remains fully extended.

Once you have hit the ball, the next logical questions are where is it going and how deep? Basically, the ball can travel in one of two directions: down the line or crosscourt. Most coaches will tell you to hit a crosscourt forehand six inches ahead of your left leg and a down-the-line six inches behind it. This is indeed roughly what happens. At the same time, your racket is laid back ever so slightly on a down-the-line, so that your wrist is just a little bit ahead of the racket head at the moment of impact, and on a crosscourt the racket head is just a bit ahead of your wrist. But during the execution of a shot you hardly have time to measure such things precisely. Instead, the simplest way of guiding the ball is to point the racket during the follow-through in the direction you want the ball to go. Merely pointing the racket during the follow-through may seem to be after the fact, but remember that the follow-through begins as soon as the racket starts to come forward, long before you actually hit the ball. If you think "crosscourt" or "down the line" as you prepare to hit the ball and are able to point the racket in the direction where you want the ball to go, all the small technical adjustments that have to be made during the forward part of the swing will pretty much take care of themselves.

Now as for depth, ideally every ground stroke should land approximately three feet from your opponent's base line and two feet from his sideline. This is, of course, patently impossible for beginners and world-class players alike, but again, the things I want to emphasize here are concentration and confidence. Aim for that base line on every shot. It's a long way away, and besides, it's better to hit too long than too short. Once you reach the stage where you can hit forehands and backhands with a fair amount of consistency, you should plan in advance where every one of your shots is going. I cannot emphasize this enough. Do it even in practice, because if you spend all of your practice time just slopping the ball back down the middle and shallow you may get a temporary satisfaction, but in a match-play situation you will find it extremely difficult to aim for the corners with confidence, let alone hit them. Being able to place the ball with accuracy and speed is vitally important if you want to become anything more than just an average player. So concentrate on direction and control right from the beginning. You won't be sorry.

Spin is what gives a shot most of its control, much in the same way as the rotation imparted to a football allows a quarterback to control a forward pass. Depending entirely on the type and amount of spin, there are three distinct kinds of forehands.

1. *The flat drive.* This is the shot I have been describing up to now. The racket face is perfectly perpendicular

to the ground at the moment of impact and the ball carries over the net with a minimum of spin.

2. *The topspin drive.* This type of shot is hit with overspin. To apply it, drop the racket head just slightly during the backswing, then during the forward part of the swing roll the racket head over the top of the ball and end your follow-through slightly higher than I have shown in Figure 3D. This gives a distinct top, or forward, spin to the ball, and its trajectory will be more rounded than that of the flat drive. The flat drive clears the net by from one to two feet; the topspin drive clears it by more and thus gives a greater margin of error. The danger with this shot is that there is a tendency to put too much spin on the ball, with the result that it hangs in the air and gives your opponent a split second more time to run it down—and that can be disastrous. But it is an important shot and, when hit properly, is extremely effective. Work hard on it.

3. *The slice drive.* To hit this shot, tilt the racket face backward at nearly a forty-five-degree angle from the perpendicular. A marked underspin, or backspin, will be put on the ball. Generally speaking, this is a shot to avoid as much as possible, especially on the forehand side. Although it is perhaps the easiest shot of all to control, if it is not hit perfectly the ball tends to hang, or float, in the air. Against a net rusher this is suicide, and against anybody it is extremely difficult to hit with any pace.

The topspin and slice forehands, though, are valuable additions to your repertoire, and after you have the flat drive under control you should work hard at developing the other two. But regardless of what shot you hit, remember that the basic rules still hold. The swing should not deviate from the linear until the moment of impact, and the follow-through should be long and fluid and out toward the net in the direction where you want the ball to go.

There are two more variations of the forehand which I would like to mention in passing. The first is the chop, which is just what its name implies and is really nothing more than an exaggerated slice. It is characterized by a high backswing, a hurried downward swing, and a low follow-through. Under no circumstances should this be considered an offensive shot but, rather, a shot of last resort. It should be attempted only when you are so far out of position that there is no other option available to you.

The other variation is a down-the-line approach shot, popularized over twenty years ago by Jack Kramer, in which the ball is hit with pronounced sidespin (as opposed to overspin or underspin). To execute this shot, exaggerate the open stance which I described earlier in the chapter, lay back the racket so that at the moment of impact the wrist is very definitely ahead of the racket head—thus breaking one of the cardinal rules of the forehand—and keep the racket very nearly parallel to the net during the follow-through. This can be used only as a down-the-line approach shot and, once mastered, has the advantage of being extremely easy to control. Also, the ball will stay low to the ground, and when it bounces it will squirt off to your opponent's left and draw him off the court more than a flat, topspin, or even slice forehand would. The problem arises because there is a tendency to lay back your wrist so much that all power is lost from the shot and your opponent can easily run down the ball and drive it past you with great ease. It's a good shot, but don't worry about it until you've got the others down pat.

When I was just starting out, my coach told me, "Don't worry if your opponent knows where your shots are going. If they're good enough it won't make any difference." True, but you still should strive to disguise all of your shots as much as possible. There are a lot of things you can do with a forehand—hit it crosscourt, hit it down the line, drive it, loop it, slice it, hit a lob off it, et cetera—and not advertising your intentions can often make the difference between a winning and a losing shot.

Disguise is accomplished in two ways. The first is nothing more complicated than making sure your swing is the same on every shot. The position of your feet, your backswing, and even your follow-through should always be the same. The direction of a shot and its spin are determined totally by the relationship of the racket to the ball right at the moment of contact, and what you do before or after that point should change only slightly from one shot to the next. To a knowing opponent, even the smallest difference in the position of your feet or in the kind of backswing, for example, can be the same as sending him a telegram that says "a topspin crosscourt is on its way" or "here comes a slice down the line."

The second way of disguising your shots is by the extensive use of your wrist. Experimenting with "wristing" your shots should be attempted only after you reach an advanced or tournament level. Basically, the racket should be considered an extension of your arm and at the moment of impact your wrist—the connecting link between your arm and the racket—should be locked solidly in place. But even then the wrist, supple and flexible, is what allows you to make last-second corrections in your swing just before you meet the ball. As you progress, you'll find that the more you use your wrist, the later you'll be able to start your swing, and that the swing itself will be more of a flick of the wrist than a long movement of the arm. And the quicker your swing, the less time your opponent has to detect your intentions.

The Backhand

For what are mostly psychological reasons, the backhand usually presents the biggest stumbling block to a beginner's progress, and especially to that of a woman. But regardless of what you have heard, and undoubtedly have seen, as you scrutinized your friends' games, the backhand is actually an easier shot to master than the forehand. Once you believe this, the battle is half won. It is unfortunately true that most players, and again especially women, have more strength on their forehand side, but the relative simplicity of the backhand more than makes up for this deficit. The backhand is a more natural stroke because during its execution your right arm (presuming you're right-handed) is flung out and away from your body, as opposed to the forehand, where the natural rhythm of that stroke carries your arm across and into your body. The backhand stroke has been compared to a left-hander's baseball swing—in fact, that is perhaps the best way to think of it—and seen in that light there is nothing difficult at all about its execution. At the highest level of the game, most players have better backhands than forehands. We find we can get more power and accuracy with less effort and that it's the most effective shot with which to approach the net.

So forget the stories you might have heard about the difficulties of the backhand, remember what I said earlier in this chapter about learning the forehand and backhand together and spending equal time on each shot, and who knows? You'll probably end up doing what I do on occasion—run around my forehand to hit a backhand. It's a fun shot.

Like the forehand, the backhand should be hit with one continuous motion beginning from the time you determine that the ball is coming to your backhand side to the time you complete your follow-through. The shot's four main components are the same as those of the forehand—the early backswing, the maximum backswing, the moment of impact, and the follow-through— and are illustrated in Figures 4A through 4D.

In talking about the forehand, I mentioned that a slightly open stance was preferable to a perfectly closed stance, or one in which the feet are even with each other and parallel to the net. For the backhand, a closed stance is a must. Since your right arm is to the left side of your body during the early part of the swing, in order to get your shoulders perpendicular to the net with an open stance you would have to roughly assume the posture of a corkscrew. In Figure 4A, I have begun to

FIGURE 4
*The Backhand / No open
stance here. The early part
of my swing is still level
and unhurried, but my
shoulders and feet now
form a plane that is
perpendicular to the net
right up until the moment
of impact, which takes
place between twelve and
eighteen inches ahead of
my right leg.*

A

B

move into position and have started to take my racket back. Because you have less strength on this side, don't hesitate to cradle the racket gently in your left hand wherever along the handle it feels most comfortable. For most players this is right at the base of the throat.

Most of the rules I talked about in discussing the forehand apply to the backhand from this point on. The head of my racket is about waist high and will remain at that level until I hit the ball. I have slightly more weight on my back foot, but I am standing completely balanced to give myself a solid foundation from which to execute the shot.

At the moment of maximum backswing, Figure 4B, my right arm is fully extended, and the plane formed by my feet and shoulders is roughly perpendicular to the net. The head of my racket does not extend back and around me any farther than the imaginary extension of this plane. Rather, it is as though I were reaching with my right arm for something to the left and almost directly in back of me. At this point in the swing, there is one crucial difference between the forehand and the backhand. I've said that you can improve your forehand by adding a slight loop to the backswing for the sake of rhythm and timing. But on the backhand the backswing is straight back—no loops or any other kind of frill. Only if you attempt a shot with very exaggerated overspin, such as a sharp crosscourt passing shot, should you even consider a loop. It doesn't add anything to the shot and if you're not careful it can present more problems than it's worth.

The biggest difference between the forehand and backhand occurs at the moment of impact, although the theory is the same: hit the ball as far in front of you as you can. For the forehand, I said, this was approximately even with your left, or leading, leg. For the backhand, as shown in Figure 4C, this point is some twelve to eighteen inches in front of the right leg. If you have prepared properly—moved into the ball, hit it on the rise and waist high—this is the point of maximum power. Again, keep your eye on the ball right up to the exact moment of impact and beyond, and remember to hit out freely. Note that my right arm is nearly fully extended at the moment of impact, just as it was at the time of my maximum backswing. The farther away from your body that you hit the ball—assuming, of course, you still hit it in the pocket of your strings—the more power and accuracy you'll have.

Figure 4D is the follow-through, and it is a mirror image of its forehand counterpart. I have not succumbed to the tendency to wrap the racket around my neck on this shot either, but have taken a long follow-through with my racket head pointed straight out toward the net.

For some reason, beginners and champions alike tend to hit their backhands with a slight slice, probably because it's easier. This is perfectly acceptable. What I have described here is essentially a flat backhand drive, but the backhand can also be hit with topspin or underspin. In fact, neither of the two best backhands of the modern era has been hit flat. Don Budge's classic was hit with overspin, and Ken Rosewall's is hit with severe slice. But the execution of the stroke remains essentially the same, and the only difference between a flat, topspin, and slice backhand is the angle at which the racket meets the ball. If you favor either a topspin or a slice—and both should eventually become important additions to your repertoire—remember to keep your racket head level up until the moment of impact. But to hit a topspin, brush the racket over the top of the ball, and to hit a slice, tilt the racket face backward during the forward part of the swing. In either case, the most important element is a long, flowing follow-through. If you don't have this, the topspin drive will degenerate into a loopy fluff shot that won't have the necessary depth, and the slice drive will degenerate into a soft floater that will hang in the air and invite some-one with even only a mediocre volley to slam your drives down your throat.

Outside of the obvious technical differences that I've attempted to explain, nearly everything I said about the forehand applies to the backhand as well. The rules and suggestions for preparation, depth, accuracy, spin, and disguise are the same on either side. Here is a quick review of the major checkpoints you should note as you hit the forehand and backhand.

1. In the ready position, face the net with your racket held directly in front of you, waist high and parallel to the ground. Be alert. Be on the balls of your feet so that you feel tension in the calves of your legs, and be prepared to go to either your right or your left.

2. Concentrate. Don't watch your opponent or the guy on the next court or anything except the ball, especially from the time it leaves your opponent's racket to the time you hit it with yours.

3. As you move toward the ball, whether to your left or to your right, remember that you want to move sideways and *in*to the ball, not sideways and backward, and that if at all possible you want to hit it on the rise. Use your knees as elevators, especially to get down to low balls, so that you hit every ball waist high. At that height you can swing most comfortably and generate the most power.

4. During the backswing, your shoulders should be at right angles to the net. On the forehand side, a slightly open stance is allowable and even encouraged; on the backhand side, your feet should be turned sideways as well.

5. During the entire swing you should feel a definite tension through your back as your torso, in effect, first coils and then uncoils while you bring back the racket and then swing forward. The swing itself should be nearly all level; the racket head should be neither raised nor lowered at the point of maximum backswing, nor should it be raised or lowered during the forward part of the swing, but there should be a pronounced upswing after you have hit the ball.

6. At the moment of impact remember that the racket is an extension of your arm and don't crowd the ball. Use the full length of your racket and arm together. This allows you to swing more freely and generate more power.

7. Think in advance about what kind of shot you're

going to hit, how deep it's going, and where on the other side of the net it's going to land.

8. Hit the ball with confidence and force (although not at the expense of rhythm). Don't worry if at first you don't have a great deal of accuracy. Power is more important than control for a beginner, and it is much easier to add control once you have power than it is to add power to control.

9. Don't expect miracles. Rome wasn't built in a day, and tennis players aren't developed in a week, or a month, or even a year. Be patient and remember that the ground strokes are the most important building blocks for a good tennis game.

The Return of Service

Now I would like to invite you to take a careful look at a very special kind of ground stroke—the return of serve. In match play, the most important consideration is to gain control of the point. Tennis is a game of offense, and unless you are among the extremely rare breed of players who actually prefer to play defensive tennis and spend the entire afternoon counterattacking their opponents' strengths (among currently active players, Nancy Richey and Ken Rosewall come to mind as examples of this type), your objective is going to be to get the upper hand as soon as possible. Half the time, obviously, the best way to do this is through the service.

And just as obviously, the other half of the time the quickest way is through the return of service.

The return of serve is the first line of defense against what can be one of your opponent's most effective weapons, and in this era of serve-and-volley tennis, where one service break is usually enough to win a set, it deserves special consideration. In hitting the return, you have the advantage of knowing within very defined limits where your opponent is going to hit the ball, and you can gird yourself both mentally and physically to make one good shot knowing that you'll have all the time in the world to prepare for it. By the same token, there is the obvious disadvantage that you are probably going to be facing an extremely powerful shot. Thus, on both counts, a well-executed return of serve is quite possibly the most satisfying shot you can ever hit.

The first consideration is where to stand while you wait for the serve. Against any shot, and especially the service, you should position yourself so that you are equidistant between the two extreme lines of flight the ball can follow. There are two cases: when you receive service in the deuce or right-hand court, and when you receive in the advantage, or left-hand court. In the deuce court, the serve, at its widest points, can either be hit directly down the middle to your backhand or sliced wide to your forehand. Assuming that your opponent is right-handed, the natural motion of his service —from his right across his body to his left—will cause the ball to drift to your right. And you'll be surprised how much. Even on a perfectly flat serve, the natural drift, discounting spin, will carry the ball from two to four feet to the right of the extension of a line drawn from the server to where the ball bounces in the service court. (The paths of the various serves are shown in another context in Diagram 2, page 58.) And if he chooses to hit a serve with extreme slice, it may wind up a good eight to ten feet to your right and pull you practically into the adjoining court. Because of this, when you receive service in the deuce court you should position yourself so that your right foot is on the spot where the sideline and the base line join. At first it may appear that you're giving away a lot of ground to your left and are going to be hopelessly out of position for a hard, flat serve down the middle. And in fact you are. But what you lose on the left side you gain on the right by protecting yourself against that wide sliced serve, and in the end you come out ahead. If nothing else, you tempt your opponent to go for the perfect serve down the middle, and often enough that increased pressure will force him to miss his service to that side.

If he chooses to hit wide to your right, again the perfect service will be an outright winner, or at the very least force you to send up an easy return. But anything less than perfection on that side and you're in perfect position. An angled return is what you want to be able to hit in the first place (more about this in Chapter 7), and if he gives you that angle on a platter, so much the better.

In the advantage, or left-hand court, the situation is almost reversed. The natural right-to-left service motion of your opponent will still tend to make the ball drift to his left (and your right), but this drift is largely negated because the primary path the ball follows is to his right. To bring in a bit of physics, one vector force cancels the other. The chances of his getting the extreme outside angle are prohibitive, so don't worry about it. Stand about three feet in from the sideline and you again will be equidistant between the two extreme lines of flight. A service to your left cannot carry you too far off the court, and a service down the middle to your right will force you only slightly in that direction. By standing in toward the middle in the advantage court, then, you have again covered everything but the perfect service.

The second service, is, of course, a safer shot. It is generally hit with more spin to provide the higher trajectory which gives the server a greater margin of error. It is also generally not hit with as much speed, or pace. Taken together, this simply means that the ball is going to be in the air for a longer amount of time, and that in turn means you're going to have more time to plan and execute your return. Perfect. On the first service your opponent has the advantage, presuming you are of equal ability. On the second service you have an advantage over him; at the very least you are no worse than even. This is the time to attack and immediately establish control of the point.

How far in should you stand for this return? On the first service, I suggested right on the base line. This may vary by as much as a foot or two on either side, depending on the relative strengths of your opponent's service and your return, but let's presume that you do indeed stand on the base line to receive the first service. There are two theories on where to stand for the second. Most players prefer to park right on that base line until the server tosses up the ball and then, like a bounding gazelle, take two or three quick steps forward. In theory, this accomplishes two things: first, it forces the returner to move forward, which is helpful if he is attacking;

second, it is supposed to create an element of surprise. But, in reality, anybody about to hit a second service knows that one way or another his opponent (namely you) is going to be on the attack, and in my opinion, all those two or three little steps do is throw the returner off balance for when he does have to hit the ball. Preparedness is one of the keys to successful tennis. On a return of service you can take all the time you want to get prepared. Why lose the advantage by bouncing all over the court while your opponent is serving the ball? What you gain by bounding into an attack position you lose in preparedness. Any time you're in motion at the same time that the ball's moving, you're going to have a tougher time watching it, anticipating to which side it's coming, and figuring out its speed and spin.

What I recommend is to move in a foot or two before your opponent even starts his service motion. Since you're not going to surprise him by moving forward, get this out of the way in plenty of time to set yourself for the return. At the same time, you give notice that you're about to tee off on his second service. I want my opponents to see me move in. Then they know they've got to get that second service in good and deep and that if they don't, I'm going to be on top of it. I feel I'm putting pressure on them before we even start the point, and that little psychological edge can be just as important as the technical edge you already have. You accomplish everything you would accomplish by moving in while your opponent is serving, and you still give yourself the maximum time to prepare your return.

Keep one thing in mind, however. You no longer are standing on your base line, and there is suddenly less distance between you and your opponent's base line. But after you have hit a few returns from this position, it should be as easy a shot for you as any other.

There are four basic rules for hitting the return of serve.

1. Be ready. You should be well prepared any time, of course, but this is the one time when it's illegal for your opponent to hit the ball until you want him to, and you should make the most of it. Stand on the balls of your feet with your racket held firmly in front of you and pointed straight out toward the net. A hard-hit service is going to come in at you low, and there is no point holding your racket high and then having to lower it again as you start your swing. You should be prepared to hit either a forehand or a backhand, but in the ready position grip your racket for the shot you least like to hit. If your forehand isn't quite as reliable as your backhand, then wait for the service with your forehand grip. If your backhand is a bit queasy, then be prepared first of all to hit a backhand. This is only common sense. Do everything you can to make your weaker shot less difficult for you.

2. Pivot your shoulders. When I talked about the forehand and backhand, I suggested that making sure your shoulders are perpendicular to the net and coiling your torso are more important to the success of those shots than the position of your feet. The same thing is true on a return of service, only more so. When you face a really powerful service, you're not going to have time to move your feet very much anyway.

3. Against a hard service, too, it is essential that you shorten up your swing as much as possible. On a slow surface like clay, or against a soft service, you will have time to wind up and hit the return just as you would a normal ground stroke. Fine. But against a good serve on a fast court you're not going to have this luxury. Then you must either slice the return or simply block it back. Your job is to meet the ball solidly, and this means taking no backswing, or at the most a very slight one. Just stick out the racket and don't attempt to draw it back at all. If your wrist is firm and your follow-through solid, the momentum of the service will provide enough pace for your return and you'll be in pretty good shape.

4. When returning a hard service remember that your opponent has the advantage, and that your first goal is to neutralize that advantage and take the initiative away from him. This means first and foremost keeping the ball in play. The most demoralizing thing for a good server to see is that little white ball come back, in any way, shape, or form. Then, too, more than 80 percent of the points in tennis are lost through errors, not won by placements, and every time you force your opponent to hit the ball, the more the odds work in your favor. If you can't go for an outright winner, then hit the return low and slow and right at your opponent's feet. (I'm presuming a good server will also be a conscientious net rusher.) This forces him to bend over and put his own pace on the ball, which is both annoying and physically demanding. By hitting the ball softly you will have time to get in good position for his return, and if you haven't already gained the initiative, when you

hit the ball the second time you definitely will be in a position to assert your control.

In summary, the mechanics of the return of service are fairly simple. It is merely a very special kind of ground stroke hit exactly like a ground stroke, except that most of the time the swing will be shorter. Strategically, remember that the return of service determines immediately who has control of the point, you or your opponent, and that about 60 percent of the time a good return means the point will fall your way. Consider the shot as important as either your forehand or your backhand, and practice it separately from them. The technical ease of the return of service, I think, will surprise you, and the shot will be one of the great pleasures of your tennis career.

3 | The Service

If the return of service is the Maginot Line of tennis, then the service is the blitzkrieg. A hard, accurate first serve and a consistent, well-placed second serve are absolutely essential, and you must know how to hit them, especially if your goals in tennis extend beyond games with your next-door neighbor. The modern emphasis on the Big Game demands first and foremost an overpowering service. The lack of a good service won't stop you from becoming a decent player but, unless you are an extremely gifted athlete, it will eliminate the possibility of your ever reaching the ranks of the world's best. This is probably unfortunate, but with so many of the top tournaments being played on grass, fast cement, or fast composition surfaces, it is imperative that you win your service almost every time you go to the line. A good service can win points for you quickly, effortlessly, and efficiently and take a lot of pressure off the other parts of your game. Conversely, a bad service will cause the rest of your game to deteriorate, through lack of confidence if nothing else, and if it's really in bad shape, could possibly cost you a match even before you step on the court. In almost every sport the best defense is a good offense, and the serve can be the most potent offensive shot in the book.

The service is at once the easiest shot for a beginner to learn and, for an intermediate or advanced player, the most difficult to utilize effectively. It is easy to learn because hitting a serve is exactly like throwing a baseball or football, the only difference being that you "throw" the tennis ball with a racket instead of your hand. In fact, one of the best ways to get a rough idea of the service motion is to take an old racket you don't care anything about, stand on the base line, and actually hurl it into the opposite service court. If you can do that you can learn the service. Simple enough. Also, for the most part you are hitting a stationary object when you serve (or should be—I'll get to that in a minute), for the first and only time during the point. On every other shot, the ball is moving with a confusing variety of pace, spin, and direction, but on the service it's just standing up there aching to be slugged, almost like a golf ball on a tee.

The service grip, Figure 5, is the same as that for the Continental forehand, with the familiar V pointed along the upper left corner of the handle just barely to the left of where it was for my own forehand. As in the case of the forehand and backhand grips, the essential elements here are control and comfort. Eventually you may change your grip slightly; that's fine. But for now stick with the one illustrated here. It gives you a firm hold on the racket and at the same time allows you freedom to use your wrist to full advantage when you hit spin and slice services.

In Figure 6 and Figures 7A through 7D the five main phases of the service are shown. Figure 6 represents

FIGURE 5
*The Service Grip/This **is** also the grip I use for my forehand and backhand volleys. Firmness and mobility are the keys. Holding the racket this way, I can hit my flat service forcefully and at the same time use my wrist to full advantage on spin and slice services.*

FIGURE 6
The Service Ready Position/I have provided myself with a solid, mobile platform from which to hit any kind of service. My weight is evenly distributed across both legs, I am facing the net, and a line connecting my feet would form about a sixty-degree angle with the base line.

the service ready position and Figures 7A through 7D the toss, the maximum backswing, the moment of contact, and the follow-through.

To begin, take a position about twelve inches away from the center of the base line. According to the rules, of course, to serve into the deuce court, you may stand behind the base line anywhere from the center of the court to the right sideline, and to serve into the advantage court, anywhere from the center to the left sideline. But by standing as near to the center of the court as possible you immediately accomplish one of your primary goals—to be where you can best cover both sidelines on your opponent's return. Also, you are in the best position from which to rush the net, should you choose to do so—and you should. You may prefer, as some players do, to stand up to six or eight feet away from the center. This has the advantage of providing a better angle if you are serving to the outside (as opposed to down the middle), but it also gives your opponent a better angle for his return, besides leaving one sideline totally unprotected. There are instances when you should, indeed, stand farther away from the center, but these are so rare in singles play that they're not worth considering while you learn the mechanics of the service.

In Figure 6 my left foot is set about two inches behind the base line. My right foot is placed comfortably about twelve inches behind my left foot and about four inches to the right of it. A line connecting my feet would form about a sixty-degree angle with the base line. I am mostly sideways to the net but slightly facing it. The important things are that I am comfortable and mobile and have provided myself with a solid base to work from. This sounds a bit complicated, but again, imagine that you are about to throw a baseball. You should *not* be totally facing the net, nor should you be lined up so that your feet are parallel and pointed toward your right sideline. You can't throw a baseball from either of these positions; neither can you hit a tennis ball. While you hold the racket with your right hand, cradle the throat of it gently in your left, which also contains a tennis ball. Be firm, but be relaxed.

From this point on, the rest of the service should take place in a continuous, flowing motion. Once you start to throw up the ball, your racket arm should never pause until you have finished your follow-through. This is extremely important, because if you stop your swing that naturally means you have to start it again, and everything that preceded the interruption is just wasted motion. As with every other shot, the service is a series of individual actions which make up a whole, and at the time that you are executing any one of the actions you should keep the whole in mind.

One of the keys to a good service is a consistent toss. Every toss should be at the same speed, reach the same maximum height, and follow the same parabolic arc. The main problem for beginners is that they can't get the toss in the same place every time. And this is crucial. First of all, make the toss with your entire arm, and think of it as though you were lifting the ball into the air. Consider your hand an ice cream cone, if you will, and the ball a scoop of ice cream at the top of it. Hold the ball with your fingers, not with the palm of your hand. This way you have more feel, and it's much easier to release the ball. Then simply lift your left arm into the air as far as you can, and without flicking your wrist, let go of the ball. If you release the ball at the last second, then you've guided it with your arm most of the way, and the longer you can hold onto the ball and direct it with your arm, the more uniform your toss will be. The maximum height of the toss should be where your racket will be when you are stretched to your fullest height, about four feet above your head. If you let the ball fall to the ground, it should land about one foot to your right and two feet into the court in front of you.

Practice the toss by itself until you can throw the ball into the air in the same place every time, and always remember that what you want to do is hit the ball at its maximum height—not when it's still going up and not after it has started back down, but right at the top of its arc. When you can do this consistently, you will have overcome the most basic, and most difficult, part of the service motion.

Now, consider that you are standing in the middle of a clock, with high noon directly in front of you and six o'clock directly behind you. As you begin your toss, swing your racket arm in a downward arc past your right leg roughly in the direction of four-thirty until you reach the position shown in Figure 7A. Actually, if this portion of the backswing ends anywhere between three-thirty and five-thirty you're in good shape. The main point is to make sure that it does not extend around you beyond six o'clock, because if that happens you force your torso to twist violently to the right, and the forward part of the swing will have to be circular instead of straight in the direction of the net.

In Figure 7A note that I have not yet released the

FIGURE 7

The Service/ Although the service motion is shown in four different steps, it should in fact be continuous. In Figure 7B note especially the angle of my elbow and the position of my racket, and in 7C that I am fully stretched out at the moment of impact.

A

B

C

D

ball. As you bring the racket back, keep your elbow away from your body. You don't want to crowd yourself on this shot, either. Now the racket will begin to curl over your head and drop into the position shown in Figure 7B.

This is the "scratching your back" position and is the single most important element in the service motion. Let's go back to our baseball comparison. If you look at a pitcher just before he releases the ball, you'll find that his right arm is in almost exactly the same position as mine is here. This is the point of maximum backswing. Now I am fully wound up, fully coiled, and ready to release all of my pent-up strength and momentum. To attain this position in another way, take the racket in your right hand, reach over your right shoulder, and scratch the small of your back. If you do this properly, your right elbow will be almost straight up in the air, as mine is, and you will feel a slight strain in your upper arm. Also, notice that my back is perfectly straight, or if anything, arched slightly backward.

From this point, simply bring the racket forward as though you were going to hurl it to the other side of the net. When you begin the service motion, your weight should be distributed more or less equally between your two feet. Now your natural momentum will carry you forward so that at the moment of impact your right foot is nearly equal with your left. In Figure 7C I have just hit the ball. My body is fully stretched out so that it presents very nearly a straight line from the bottom of your feet to the top of my racket. My shoulders are held up throughout this part of the stroke, simply because if I do that, the rest of my body will pretty much straighten out automatically. *Don't* bend at the waist. When you start to come forward, everything should come forward at once. Bending at the waist, or anywhere else, before you hit the ball only causes you to fold over like an accordion, or a wet noodle. Keep everything rigid and moving together at the same time and in the same direction. Otherwise you lose power.

My follow-through, Figure 7D, is to the left of my body and my right foot has taken a big step toward the net. Some players have a tendency to finish their service on the right side, but if you wind up over there it means you have not used your body to the fullest and that whatever power you have generated has come almost exclusively from your arm. Besides, you're liable to clobber that right leg as your racket comes forward at the end of the swing.

All of this sounds terribly complex, but it isn't. Simplicity is, in fact, what you are trying for on every shot and it's just as easy to attain here as anywhere else. Almost without exception, the best services in tennis history, such as that of Pancho Gonzales, have been the simplest, without the jerks and gyrations that disrupt rhythm and destroy momentum. Until you get a feel for the shot, I would suggest practicing it in three stages. First, just toss the ball up in the air and coordinate the toss with the early part of your backswing (up to the position I have reached in Figure 7A) until you get a consistent rhythm established. Second, don't use a backswing at all. Place the racket in the "scratching your back" position—making sure that your elbow is pointed high in the air—then toss the ball up and proceed with the forward half of the swing. I think you'll find this is the best way to establish just what your racket does during this part of the service. Third, hit the ball using the full swing, but keep your feet planted firmly on the ground and don't worry about leaning forward into the shot. You won't be able to generate as much pace, but this is the best way I know to become aware of balance. Finally, when you feel comfortable with all of these gimmicks separately, put everything together. When you can do this without a hitch anywhere along the line, you will be well on your way to developing the potent service you need for topflight tennis.

What I have just described is the basic service motion. There are three different kinds of serves that you should learn—flat, spin, and slice—but all three are hit in essentially the same way, with only small differences in the toss and forward part of the swing, which give to each serve its particular characteristics. There should be absolutely no deviation in the backswing or, until you reach the position shown in Figure 7B, from one service to the next. Any difference during this part of the swing will telegraph your intentions even more than a change in the swing of the backhand or forehand. Now let's take a look at the three serves separately.

1. *The flat serve.* This service is exactly what its name implies. The toss should be as I described earlier —about one foot to the right and two feet in front of you—and the forward part of the swing should be straight down following the same path you would use in bringing a meat cleaver down onto a cutting block. At the moment of impact, with your arm and racket extended in a perfectly straight line above your head,

the face of the racket meets the ball squarely and no attempt is made to put any spin at all on the ball. There is, however, some natural rotation imparted as your racket and arm move across your body from right to left. The presence of this slight spin, which means that the serve can never be truly flat, is what gives you control. In the beginning, in fact, you should consciously add more of this spin to your "flat" serve, and you can do it by merely twisting your wrist just a hair to the right (so that your racket face points just slightly to the left) at the moment of impact. But, don't forget, after you have hit the ball, still bring your racket straight forward and down during the follow-through.

Keep in mind that this is nothing more than a device to help you learn control. The more you turn your wrist, the less power you can generate, and the object of the flat service is power.

The flat serve is your first serve—the blockbuster—and should be successful at least two-thirds of the time. Anything less than that and you're going to find yourself in deep strategic trouble, not to mention the fact that all those missed first serves will rapidly tire you. A good first serve takes a lot out of you, and for it to be effective it must be consistent as well as hard.

2. *The spin serve.* The most inexcusable error in tennis is the double fault. It gives your opponent something for nothing, and besides the immediate advantage on the scoreboard, provides him with a tremendous psychological boost. (It doesn't do a whole lot for your frame of mind, of course.) This shot, your primary second service, should be the guarantee that you don't give away points cheaply. The first service can be

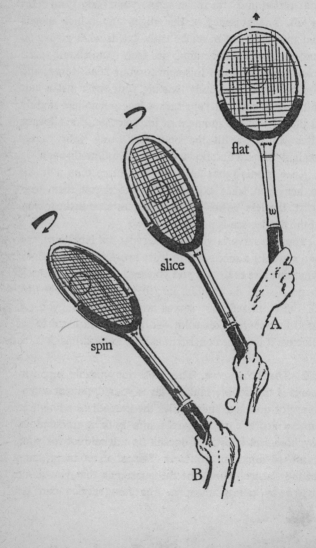

DIAGRAM 1/The moment of impact for the flat (A), spin (B), and slice (C) services

something of a gamble because you've always got one left, but the second service—the spin service—should be as nearly infallible as you can make it.

If hit properly, your first service will clear the net by around two feet and land within three feet (top players shoot for one foot) of the service line. The object of your second service is to increase significantly that rather shaky margin of error. It is extremely easy to hit a serve without any pace at all that will always go in, but all this does is provide your opponent with a chance to hit an easy return and accomplishes nothing for you. The trick is to hit the ball so that it clears the net not by one or two feet, but by around four, and lands in the opposite service court with plenty of room to spare—but still with enough pace and depth so that your opponent can't move in on it too much. The application of topspin is what allows you to do this.

The spin service differs from the flat service in two ways. First, the toss, instead of being in front and slightly to the right of you, should be almost directly overhead; in fact, if you let the ball drop it should hit you on the forehead. At its maximum height, then, the ball is approximately eighteen inches behind where it was on the flat serve. With the ball in this position, as your racket arm comes forward your back will arch back more, and your body will not tend to lean forward nearly as much as it did on the flat service. The second difference between the two serves is in this forward swing. As your racket comes up from its "scratching your back" position, strike the ball on its back side, that is, the side away from the net. And then, using your wrist, roll the face of the racket up and over the top of the ball. Although the end of your follow-through is the same, you are now hitting more up and out on the ball than you did with the flat service. This provides the extreme topspin that causes the ball to travel in a more pronounced arc on its way to the opposite side of the net and usually gives you a safe, consistent serve.

3. *The slice serve.* This is a serve which has sidespin. The toss is the same or slightly to the right of that for a first, or flat, serve. During the forward part of the swing, turn your wrist slightly to the right, and exaggerate the natural right-to-left motion of your normal service swing.

This service is extremely easy to hit and control, and when it bounces it will tend to slide off to your opponent's right. It has a significant strategic value as a means of drawing your opponent off the court (when you are serving from the deuce court) and as an element of surprise, but it cannot be hit with much pace and therefore should be used sparingly. If your opponent anticipates the slice serve, or if you don't place it perfectly, he can move in quickly and take the attack away from you with one good return.

A fourth kind of service, about which you may sometimes hear, is the American twist. In this serve the racket meets the ball on its lower left surface, comes up and over it and ends far out to the right of the body. The serve curves from right to left, but when it bounces it kicks high and to the right—that is, to your opponent's backhand. The American twist requires immense strength to execute, and is extremely awkward and difficult to control. It is probably best left alone.

To get a better visual idea of what happens during the serve, take a look at Diagrams 1 and 2. Diagram 1 is the schematic representation of how the racket meets the ball for each of the three serves I have described. Diagram 1A is the flat serve. Diagram 1B is the spin serve, emphasizing the manner in which the racket face rolls over the top of the ball. Diagram 1C is the slice serve, and shows the application of sidespin.

Diagram 2 details the paths of flight for the three serves. The line marked A shows the nearly flat trajectory of the flat service. Line B indicates the higher trajectory of the spin service and its subsequent higher bounce. Line C shows how the slice serve stays low to the ground after its bounce and skids off to the receiver's right (or to the server's left).

For some reason—I suspect that it is mostly psychological—beginners have a terrible time hitting serves with the proper depth. And by the proper depth, as I said earlier, I mean to within three feet of the service line. If the ball lands any shorter than that, you're extending an invitation for your opponent to take two steps forward and really slug the ball, probably past you for a winner. (The only possible exception is on a slice service, when your main objective is not to overpower your opponent but to surprise him by your change of pace or to pull him out of position.) The difficulty is caused by the natural fear of hitting the service too long, but a simple exercise will, in fact, show you just how difficult this is. Sometime when you're practicing, deliberately try and hit the fence—that's right, the fence—behind the other half of the court. Unless you really wind up and go wild, that's a

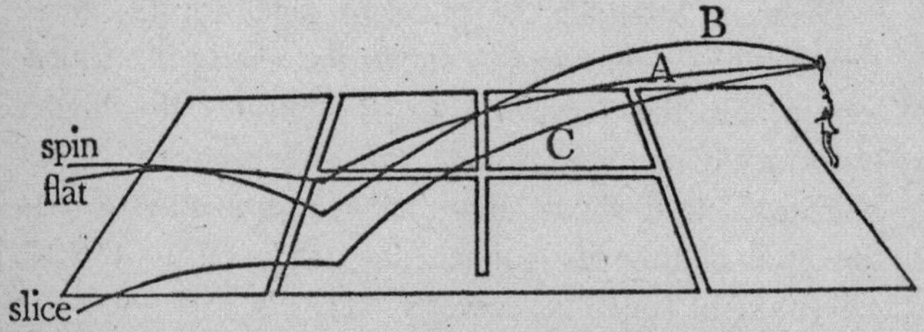

spin
flat
slice

A
B
C

DIAGRAM 2/The trajectories of the flat, spin,
and slice services

pretty difficult thing to do. When you're starting out, don't be afraid if your serves land a little behind the service line. As with the other shots, once your serve is grooved it's much easier to shorten the length of it by a foot or two than it is to gain a foot or two of depth. Most important, the more depth you can get, the more time you have to follow your service to the net, and conversely, the less time your opponent has to get set, wind up and hit his return.

You should decide where you want to hit each service before you start your service motion. This is true of every shot, but the service is the one time when you can hit the ball free of any outside influences, and you should take full advantage of the opportunity to decide where you're going to hit it. Don't give away your intentions. As I have already suggested, one way is to develop a uniform swing for all three serves. A second way is not to look where you intend to serve. This may seem an obvious point, but a surprising number of players look to their opponent's forehand or backhand side just before they begin their toss and then rather foolishly hit the ball to that same side. You have to look somewhere, of course, just to get your bearings and bring your depth perception into play, but you should train yourself to look at exactly the same place on the other side of the net before every serve—preferably right at your opponent. If you do this, and if you have a uniform swing, there is no way your opponent can tell where the ball is going until it leaves your racket.

Where you serve is governed by three factors. The first is any obvious weakness or overwhelming strength your opponent might have. If he has a devastating forehand you'll naturally avoid it and serve to his backhand most of the time. If he can't handle spin serves, then obviously you'll hit spin serves a disproportionate amount of the time. But these are special cases. More generally, where you serve is determined by the angles available to you (I mentioned this briefly while talking about the return of serve) and, surprisingly, the height of the net. At the center of the court the net is three feet high, but it increases gradually in height until at the sidelines it reaches three feet, six inches. And that six-inch difference can present all sorts of problems if you're not careful.

From the deuce court, the majority of your first serves should be hit right down the middle—down the T—to your opponent's backhand. The ball will clear the lowest part of the net, allowing you to hit it harder and flatter than if you served to the outside, and at the same time it will follow the straightest and shortest line to your opponent's service court, which means he will have less time to prepare his return. Besides, more often than not your opponent's weak side will be his backhand.

The objective of your second service—more spin and less power—is not to overpower your opponent but to get the ball in play. One of the most effective places to hit a good spin service is right at your opponent. Since you will rarely win the point outright, the next best thing is to try and tie him up. The more you can force him to take a cramped swing, the less likelihood there is of a powerful, aggressive return.

The slice service is an important weapon, but as I said earlier, should be used sparingly since its success depends almost entirely on surprise. It should be hit only as a change of pace, or if you are almost certain your opponent is anticipating a serve to his backhand.

The rules are pretty much the same from the advantage side—with two important exceptions. The slice service should be avoided almost entirely. You can't draw your opponent off the court if you hit it to his backhand, and you can't get it past him for a clean ace if you hit it to his forehand. The only possible use the slice service has from this side is if your opponent is standing a little too far over to his left. Then a slice down the middle, although it probably won't be an outright winner, will at least help keep him honest.

Again, your most powerful first service will be down the middle, but from the advantage side this means hitting to your opponent's forehand, which you probably won't want to do. So hit to his backhand, but when you do, remember that the ball is going to go over a higher part of the net than it did from the deuce side. Raise your sights a little and put a bit more topspin on the ball to make sure it gets over that barrier.

4 | The Volley

A good service without a good volley is like a gun without ammunition—useless. It's nice once in a while when you ace your opponent and win a point outright on your serve, but most of the time he's going to be able to return it, by hook, crook, or skill, and then you're going to have to hit something else to win the point. That "something else" should be the volley. If you don't have a good volley, you're naturally not going to want to rush the net anytime, and all your service will be good for is to put the ball in play in the hope you can force the attack sufficiently with your ground strokes. Sometimes, of course, this is necessary, especially if you're playing on a slow surface like clay, where much of the power of a service is absorbed by the softness of the court, but on fast surfaces like grass and cement you will want to play the classic modern game—a big, hard serve followed by a good, crisp volley or two—because if you don't your opponent undoubtedly will. And, all other things being equal, the player who attacks the most on a fast surface will have a decided advantage.

In my opinion, a serve-and-volley game is essential

for four reasons. First, by keeping you on the attack it does wonders for your confidence and general frame of mind, at the same time serving notice to your opponent that you mean business. Second, it provides a means of ending points quickly and efficiently without long and occasionally frustrating backcourt rallies as well. Third, if you are playing on an uneven surface, such as grass, by hitting the ball in the air you eliminate the possibility of bad bounces. Fourth, on windy days a volley is much easier to control than a ground stroke. In short, the volley is the most efficient shot in tennis.

As with the service, the volley is extremely easy to learn but difficult to master thoroughly. Because you generally have only half the time to prepare for a volley that you do for a ground stroke, it requires more precise timing, quicker reflexes, and better all-round coordination than any other shot. A player who can learn a good volley will generally be able to learn good ground strokes; but it does not necessarily follow that a player with solid but mechanical ground strokes will be able to execute a first-class volley. So don't be fooled by its seeming simplicity. Be more precise, more dogmatic; don't be quite as anxious to experiment.

The Continental forehand grip (also the service grip) is used for both the forehand and the backhand volleys. It will seem slightly awkward at first, but during a fast exchange at the net you don't want to have to worry about switching grips, and besides, this grip is about halfway between the forehand and the backhand grips used by most players in the first place. As with the ground strokes and service, however, comfort and feel are the primary considerations and once you have acquired enough experience and self-knowledge, don't hesitate to experiment—at least a little bit. If you decide on a grip other than the one I recommend, don't worry about it, as long as you can get the racket around fast enough to hit a solid shot from either side.

Before getting to the execution of the volley, let me emphasize the importance of position to the success of the shot. The volley should always be considered—next to the serve—your prime offensive weapon and should always be used to further your attack. The closer you are to the net, the more effective your volley is going to be, and so the cardinal rule of good volleying is to get in as close to the net as possible before each shot. For the first volley after a service, this means to within two or three feet of the service line. If you come in behind a ground stroke you should position yourself two or three feet behind the service line. After the first volley, from wherever it might be, always move forward and never stand still or retreat. From inside the service line every foot you can move forward increases tremendously the angles available to you, and the sharper the angle, the better your chances will be of hitting a putaway volley.

As you advance, however, remember to stop your forward movement completely at the moment your opponent hits his return shot, because you don't want to be caught moving in any direction until you're sure where your opponent is going to hit the ball. So whether you advance behind a ground stroke, a serve, or a volley, run in as far as you can and then get set in the ready position shown in Figure 8.

This is exactly the same ready position I described for the ground strokes and the return of service. But when you are at the net you have less time to prepare

FIGURE 8

The Volley Ready Position/I am poised on the balls of my feet with my racket held waist high in front of me and level with the ground. From this position I am ready to move quickly to my left or to my right, advance forward, or even shuffle backward to get under a well-hit lob.

for and execute a shot, so everything I emphasized in those discussions takes on added meaning now and deserves a review. You should be on the balls of your feet with your weight equally distributed on both legs and be prepared to move in any direction. If you favor one leg, say the right, and your opponent hits to your left, you'll have to take an extra step before you can turn around and go after the ball. On a ground stroke this is usually only annoying; on a return of service it's dangerous; and on a volley it's fatal. Note that my racket is pointed directly in front of me and is held low—about waist high—and level with the ground. Any ball hit hard must be low to the ground if it is to land inside the court, and this is the shot you should be first prepared to hit. If your opponent's shot has a high trajectory it must be hit with less pace if it is to land safely, and you will have plenty of time to raise your racket into position to hit it.

There is one further point here which does not apply to either the ground strokes or the return of service. At the net you must always consider the possibility of a lob (which is another reason why you should not be caught moving forward as your opponent swings at the ball). Again, balance is the key. You should be prepared to move to your left or right with equal quickness, but at the same time you should be ready to shuffle backward if necessary. This is, however, more a matter of mental alertness than anything else and should not lessen your desire to move forward.

In most cases you'll be able to see a lob coming a split second or two before your opponent actually hits it. An offensive or topspin lob, which I'll talk about in a later chapter, is difficult to disguise; a defensive lob is nearly impossible to hide. Besides, if worse comes to worst, you can always retreat and run down all but the best lobs with just a little extra effort. Once you've pressed your attack you should never hang back in an effort to protect yourself against what 75 percent of the time is strictly a defensive shot anyway. Once you start to do that, you're liable to spend too much of your time in no man's land, that awkward area halfway between the base line and the service line, where you're too far back to really hit a good volley and too close in to hit a solid ground stroke. You should always be aware of the possibilities of a lob, but not to the point where it causes you to forget your primary goal, which is to get to that net and attack. If you haven't won the point by the third volley, the chances are good that you're going to be in a vulnerable, defensive posture and will probably lose the exchange.

When you see where your opponent has hit the ball, continue forward to meet it as far as you can go—don't wait for the ball to come to you—and as you start your swing turn your body in the direction of the ball by stepping forward and across your body with the opposite foot. If the ball is to your right, step forward and cross your body with your left foot (don't step backward with your right); if the ball is on your backhand side, step forward and across with your right foot. Your shoulders and feet should both be parallel to the net on either side because you want to hit the ball as far in front of you as possible—about a foot ahead of your left leg on the forehand and two feet ahead of your right leg on the backhand—and you simply can't do that if any part of you is facing the net.

The forehand volley swing is shown in Figures 9A

A

B

FIGURE 9
The Volley/I have taken practically no backswing, and the distance my racket travels forward before it meets the ball is no more than two feet. The fore-hand volley motion is not so much a swing as it is a punch, and the same thing is true, in mirror image, for the backhand.

C

through 9C. The backhand volley is in every way a mirror image of the forehand.

The most important thing to know about the backswing for a volley is that there is hardly any. You don't really swing at a volley. It's more like a punch, like a neat right cross in boxing, and the distance the racket moves forward before it hits the ball is no more than two feet. There are three reasons for this short swing. First, the shorter the swing, the more racket control you have. Second, much of the power you need at the net for an effective volley comes from the force of your opponent's drive anyway, and you can easily supply the rest within that two-foot swing. Third, most of the time you're just not going to have time to take a full swing. At first you'll have a tendency to take a full backswing just as you would for a ground stroke, but if you learn to punch your volleys from the very beginning you'll never have to worry about breaking a bad habit. A swinging volley is a very spectacular shot when it works. But it rarely works. So just do what I have done in Figure 9A and extend your racket no farther back than your back shoulder (in this picture, my right shoulder). Make sure that your wrist is firm, and then swing—punch. That's all there is to it.

Most of the volleys you hit will be at a height somewhere between your waist and your shoulder. For every volley in this range your swing should be LEVEL. It seems that everybody is taught to hit down on a volley with the racket head laid back so that extreme underspin is put on the ball. This kind of swing is easier, results in a more safely hit ball, and is extremely incorrect. You want power and depth on a volley just as much as you want them on your ground strokes, and you simply can't get either if you slice the ball too much. Volleys hit in this power range should be hit almost flat, with just a touch of underspin. At the moment of impact—Figure 9B—notice that my racket head is nearly perpendicular to the ground even though I am hitting the ball well in front of me. And during the follow-through—Figure 9C—my racket is pointed "up and out" much in the same way as it was on my forehand follow-through. If you hit a volley with a high backswing and a low follow-through, the lessened pace will allow your opponent to run down volleys that might otherwise be winners.

Note also in Figure 9C that although my backswing is short, almost nonexistent, my follow-through is still rather long. The ball stays on the strings for at least six inches of the volley swing, too, during which time the ball receives its direction and control, and you shouldn't slap at this shot any more than you should slap at a ground stroke. A firm wrist is essential.

What I have described is pretty much the ideal volley—one that you can hit at a height somewhere between your waist and your shoulders and close to your body. Unfortunately, your opponent isn't likely to cooperate and hit every shot into this power range, and you will have to make some quick technical adjustments in order to hit a solid, forcing shot. There are four distinct kinds of volleys that fall outside of this power range—the wide volley, the low volley, the high volley, and the tight volley, one in which the ball comes right at you.

The problem presented by a wide volley is that, beyond a point, the more you have to stretch out to meet the ball, the less power you can generate. Then it becomes even more important for you to make sure you hit up and out on the ball, even if you have to take a slightly longer backswing than I recommended originally. But, remember, you're not going to have a great deal of time to get ready for the shot. Keep your wrist firm no matter how far you have to reach, and still remember to hit the ball as far in front of you as possible.

Whenever possible, volleys should not be hit any lower than the level of your waist. But when the ball comes at you low and hard and maybe even dips a little when it crosses the net to your side of the court, you will have to get down for it. Although your racket will then be well below waist level, it should be kept parallel to the ground at the moment of impact. This means you have got to bend those knees even more than you would for a low ground stroke.

In Figure 10 I have chosen to illustrate a low backhand volley even though the general rules apply to either side. Note that although I am bending from the waist, my knees are the primary elevators that allow me to get low to the ground, and that the head of my racket is nearly level with my forearm.

Then consider where the head of my racket is, namely below the level of the net. I said earlier that you should hit every volley almost flat, but if I did that now I would hit the ball smack into the net. On a low volley, then, I've got to get under the ball and slice it just a little bit to get it up and over the net. I have done this by laying back the racket head so that it meets the ball at a slight angle. As you swing, take less backswing than you would on a normal volley. On a low volley you can't generate as much power as you

FIGURE 10

The Low Backhand Volley/ A low volley should be hit with your racket parallel to the ground. I am bending primarily from my knees— as I would for a low backhand—and my racket head is tilted back at a slight angle to help me boost the ball up and over the net.

can on one that is waist high to begin with, and by slicing the ball you lose a good bit of depth. So on both counts you must compensate by swinging more in an upward direction during follow-through.

A high volley presents the same problems in reverse. A volley hit above the height of the shoulder, especially on the forehand side, is, for two reasons, one of the most difficult shots in tennis. The first, believe it or not, is that you have too much time to hit the ball. If this seems strange, consider that on most of your volleys you have about half as much time to get set as you do for a ground stroke, and once you have mastered the fundamentals of the volley, much of what you do at the net is strictly reflex. You get used to a certain rhythm by hitting two or three hard volleys in a row and if, suddenly, you have to prepare for a shot coming at you significantly more slowly (which a high ball will do), the rhythm is thrown all off. Instead of swinging by instinct and reflex, you've got to stand there waiting for the ball; if you're not careful this wait can throw off your entire rhythm. The second reason that a high volley is difficult is that a ball above the height of your shoulders can't be hit with much strength in either the horizontal or the vertical plane. There just isn't any way to hit a ball up there with a lot of pace unless you really swing at it, and as I said before, a swinging volley is very spectacular but very unreliable.

Once you've readjusted your sights, the first thing you should do is consider whether you can get under the ball quickly enough to hit it as an overhead. If you can't, then grit your teeth and hang on. Whatever you do, don't hit down on the ball. Hit straight through it, and unless you're superstrong, the ball will land in your opponent's court with plenty of room to spare. Take a little more backswing—not a full one, however, but one about halfway between a normal volley and a ground stroke. Keep your wrist extremely firm, and hit the ball flat or, if you prefer, with a slight topspin.

Fortunately, this is not a shot you will be required to hit very often, but when you have to, a little quick footwork may be able to eliminate most of its problems. Since a ball shoulder high or above is indeed going to be coming at you relatively slowly, this is the perfect time to apply one of the cardinal rules of volleying and move in as quickly and as far as you can, even if you wind up on top of the net, before you start your swing. If you're in that close, even the most awkward shot can be turned into a quick putaway, and after all, that's the main purpose of the volley in the first place.

The tight volley is nearly as much of a problem as the other three. If a ball is hit directly at you so hard that you don't have time to get out of the way, you're obviously in trouble—you're handcuffed. But you can extricate yourself most of the time if you remember three things. First, always hit a tight volley with a backhand volley swing; there's no way you can bring the racket in front of you if you hit the ball with a forehand. Second, since you won't be able to take any backswing at all, concentrate only on meeting the ball solidly. Third, because depth is also out of the question, angle the volley sharply to either side to at least force your opponent to do some running.

5 | The Overhead

In the next chapter I will suggest that a lob can be a pretty devastating weapon on occasion. But the one shot that can beat a good lob is a better overhead. When the two are paired the issue should never be in doubt. The overhead—the slam, the smash—is the knockout punch of tennis and should be considered nothing less. But before I talk in detail about the execution of this shot, I would like to mention one thing. At the highest level of the game, players never—and I mean *never*—miss the opportunity to put away a weak shot by their opponent. They don't mess around, they don't try to be cute, and they don't overhit. They just put the ball away, neatly and decisively. Period. And on the overhead more than on any other shot, you're going to have the opportunity to finish off points without any pain. Be merciless if you have to. Be brutal. But make sure that when you've got that nice easy cripple and an open court to hit into, you don't flub the shot. The ability to put away the easy shots all the time is one of the biggest differences between good players and those who are only mediocre.

The first rule for a successful overhead is: don't let

the ball get behind you. Once you determine that your opponent has thrown up a fairly decent lob, begin to move backward at once. You've got a lot of time to prepare for this shot, and the theory that applies here is the same dictating what a baseball outfielder does when he sees a high fly ball coming his way. Immediately he takes four or five steps backward—more than are necessary—because it's easier for him to move forward during those last crucial split seconds just before he catches the ball than it is to move backward. Likewise, on a tennis court you can't hit an effective overhead if at the last moment you suddenly have to backpedal. But you can hit a strong shot even if you take a step or two forward just before you hit the ball. Besides, some of your strength on the overhead comes, just as it does on the service, from leaning forward. When you see the ball coming, take as many steps backward as you need so that any last-second adjustments will be in the direction of the net, not away from it. At the same time, always keep your eye on the ball. To do both of these things at the same time means you'll actually be moving with a sort of side shuffle, with your body always sideways to the net and your left shoulder more or less pointed directly at the ball. This may sound complicated, but for up to five or six steps it's the best way to move without losing visual contact with the ball.

From then on, the overhead swing is almost an exact duplicate of the service swing, and nearly everything I talked about then applies now. There are two equally good ways to make the actual swing. The first is to cock your racket in the "scratching your back" position when you first see the lob coming, and then hold everything until the ball drops low enough for you to swing forward. The second is to keep your racket forward in the "service ready" position and make the entire swing from beginning to end with one continuous motion. I prefer the second method over the first, because it helps me establish my timing and rhythm. But I don't want to be dogmatic about it. Try both ways for yourself, and see which is more suited to you.

Whichever way you choose, as the lob falls you should be in a position so that the ball would hit you squarely on the forehead if you didn't swing your racket. Then as you swing you'll make contact with the ball at approximately the same place you would if you were hitting a service. When you come forward and actually hit the ball, make sure your feet are planted firmly on the ground. There are many spectacular pictures of players hitting overheads with both feet off the ground and their bodies going every which way, and there are even a few good players who prefer to hit the ball like this, but it usually means either that the player's opponent sent up a very good lob and he has had to hit the ball behind him, or that he simply misjudged the ball and had to make a violent correction at the last second. As your racket comes forward, hit the ball as flat as possible with perhaps just a tiny amount of slice, or sidespin, for control, and during the follow-through hit down on the ball as though you wished to drive the ball into the ground. Which, in theory, you indeed do.

Hit every overhead as deep as you possibly can. A shallow overhead will bounce nearly straight up in the air and give your opponent time to run down what should be an outright placement. Also, hit most overheads to your opponent's backhand side. Of course, don't be foolish and hit the ball over there if he's standing on his left sideline waiting for it, but it's generally easier to hit an overhead to your right than it is to hit one to your left, because to hit crosscourt you have to twist awkwardly so that your upper body is facing the net more than it should. Besides, in most match-play situations where you have a chance to put away an overhead, it won't make any difference where you place the ball, and not having to debate with yourself over the direction of the shot is just one less thing to worry about.

Always hit an overhead before it bounces. This may seem like an obvious remark, but you'd be surprised at the number of players who get cold feet on just an average lob and let it fall to the ground rather than hit it in the air. At the very least an overhead should be a means to continue your attack, and at best it is a way to end the point. Don't get nervous and hold back. All you're doing is giving your opponent a breather, or worse yet, an opportunity to counterattack. If there's any doubt at all in your mind as to what you should do, stop thinking about it and hit the ball as soon as you can.

There are two exceptions to this rule. If your opponent sends up a towering lob, one that's really going to bring rain, then drop it—let it bounce. If a lob is that high you won't lose any of your advantage by waiting a little longer to swing at it, because the ball will bounce high enough for you still to hit it fully extended, and at any rate, your opponent will have plenty of time to get back into position even if you do hit it in the air. Also, if it's a particularly windy day, a lob caught in a current of air may do all sorts of weird things on the way down that will make it difficult for you to swing from a solid base. And if you're standing near a sideline, a ball that looks as though it might land in just might float a bit and land outside the court (or, I should warn, vice versa). In any case, if things appear to be getting out of hand, let the ball bounce and regroup your forces. A word of warning: bouncing a lob gives you plenty of extra time to prepare for an overhead, but all that waiting can, if you're not careful, produce all sorts of anxiety, which might easily cause you to hurry your shot and mis-hit it. If you let an overhead drop, remember to relax. The ball isn't going to run away. Just take a deep breath and swing with the same relaxed but firm motion you would use if you were picking the ball out of the air.

If, unfortunately, everything does go wrong and you commit yourself to swinging at a lob that is obviously too far behind you or otherwise out of alignment, there is only one way to save the shot, and that's by hitting a defensive overhead. The phrase seems contradictory, but it simply means keeping the ball in play without attempting to make the shot decisive. Use the same swing you would use for a normal overhead, but don't swing quite as hard—your only consideration is to meet the ball and hit it back across the net as deeply as you can—and don't follow through. Stop your swing as soon as you make contact with the ball. If you're lucky, the ball will go back deep enough so that you can still stay in the point; if it doesn't, chalk up the mishap to experience.

There are two other aspects of the overhead that I would like to mention in passing. The first concerns the backhand overhead. As in the case of a high volley (on either side), the first rule here is to avoid the shot if at all possible. Many players can bounce a normal overhead over the fence, but there has been only one player in the modern history of the game—Tony Trabert—who could bounce a backhand overhead that hard; the shot is best avoided. Do everything in your power to move under the ball enough so you can hit it as a normal overhead on your forehand side. But if you can't, just let the ball drop low enough so you can hit it exactly as you would a high backhand volley.

Second, if you see that your opponent's lob is indeed going to land behind you before you can swing at it, don't give up on the point but immediately turn your back on the net and run—don't backpedal, shuffle, or walk, but *run*—in a straight line to the approximate area where the ball will land. If you don't have time to get around squarely behind the ball, return it the best way you can, which will probably mean with a lob. But if you do get the ball in time to set yourself, then consider the rest of the shot as nothing more than another overhead, which you have let bounce. Swing in exactly the same manner as you would for any other overhead, remembering, of course, that instead of being perhaps eighteen feet from the net you are now probably more than thirty feet away from it and can't hit down on the ball quite as sharply. Hit the ball with a slight slice, and put a lot of power into your swing. Your target area—your opponent's base line—is now over seventy feet away and you'll really need to raise your sights and muscle the ball to get the proper depth.

6 | The Trimmings

The shots I talked about in the last four chapters—forehand, backhand, return of service, service, volley, and overhead—are the basic weapons of tennis. How well you master them will determine, in the main, your eventual level of excellence. Of course, it's only natural that all of your strokes won't develop at the same rate of speed. Even the best players have pet shots, ones they prefer to hit and that are far superior to all others in their repertory. Fine. But except as I have indicated, all of these basic shots are pretty much of equal importance, and I cannot think of a single player, male or female, who has reached the highest rung of the tennis ladder without being able to execute all of them at least adequately.

The five shots that I will describe in this chapter—the lob, half volley, drop shot, drop volley, and lob volley—are so much icing on your tennis cake. Without them you can play a very respectable game and no apologies necessary, but to become a truly well-rounded player, and hence the best, you need these five shots almost as much as you need the basic six.

One of the most important strategic objectives in

tennis, which I'll talk about in more detail in Chapter 7, is to break up your opponent's rhythm, and these shots are among the best ways to do it. Ninety percent of the shots you hit during a match will be the basic six, but an occasional well-timed lob or deftly executed drop shot is often as effective as a booming service or a scathing forehand drive. Even if these shots aren't outright winners, the mere threat of them gives your opponent just one or two more things to worry about. While all of these shots can be used in both offensive and defensive situations, the lob and half volley are primarily defensive weapons, while the drop shot, drop volley, and lob volley are basically just a means to give your game that special flavor. If you can sufficiently confuse and annoy your opponent—and these shots will do both—half the battle is won.

Just one word of warning. Under no circumstances should any of these shots be considered substitutes for the game's basic weapons. Many players, especially juniors, become so enamored of certain of these shots that they use them when they should be hitting normal ground strokes and volleys. These shots are effective largely because they are used sparingly and come as a surprise, and if you keep hitting the same surprise, no matter how well it's executed it's no longer a surprise.

The Lob

The lob is perhaps the most underrated shot in tennis. Beginners and intermediate players especially shy away from it, but even among world-class players there are a few who don't use the shot nearly enough. I suppose they avoid it because they think it's silly to throw the ball up in the air when they could attempt a passing shot (a ground stroke hit past an opponent at the net, rather than over him), and actually most of the time they're right. But the next time you watch a match between two really great players notice how much they utilize the lob. I think you'll be surprised. It's very much a legitimate shot, and while there is the danger of overuse, the greater danger is not using it enough.

There are basically three kinds of lob—the offensive, the defensive, and the topspin—and their different trajectories are shown in Diagram 3.

Although an offensive lob may occasionally be an outright winner, it is usually used simply to break up the rhythm of your opponent's game. Occasionally, you'll find that a player will tend to lob a lot during the first three or four games of a match in situations where it would be just as easy to attempt a passing shot, then will lob only occasionally the rest of the afternoon. There is a good reason for this. Timing an overhead is difficult at best, and early in the match the chances are your opponent isn't fully warmed up, doesn't really feel comfortable hitting overheads, and will mis-hit—or at least hit softly—more than he puts away. Then if you lay off the lob at just about the time he starts to groove his overhead, when you do get around to throwing one up again he will have to go through the whole process of reestablishing his rhythm from scratch.

The offensive lob is hit with essentially the same motion as either the forehand or the backhand drive, although there are two important points of difference. The backswing is the same as for either ground stroke, but as you come forward with your swing, drop the racket head just slightly, and after you hit the ball follow through so that your racket is about head high at the end of your swing. This will give the ball enough loft to get up in the air.

The perfect offensive lob (Line B) is one that just clears the top of your opponent's outstretched racket, forces him to retreat from the net, and lands about three feet from the base line. But if you're really out of position you're not going to have time even to consider such niceties. In a situation like this, when you either have been pulled off the court or otherwise can't take a good swing at the ball, you should hit a defensive lob (Line A). Don't try to be cute, or even accurate. Just hit the ball as high as you can—really bring rain—but still hit the shot with as much depth as you can muster. This shot won't be a winner, but if you really sky the ball it should allow you time to recover your balance and get back to the center of the court. And who knows? A ball hit that high is accelerating quite rapidly by the time it nears the ground and the chances are good that your opponent is not going to risk hitting the ball in the air. If he lets it bounce, although you won't exactly have put him on the defensive you will have made him hesitate a little bit and forced him to hit a good overhead to win the point. Every little bit helps.

Whenever you have time—this applies to the offensive and defensive lobs equally—lob wide to your opponent's forehand. Most players find it much more difficult to run backward and to their right to get under a lob than to move back and to their left. I'm not sure why, but it just seems to be more awkward. Don't take this as the gospel truth because you'll surely run across some guy who is like lightning to his right and can't move to his left at all. But of the players I've played against, lobbing to the right side seems to be the thing to do.

Now for the topspin lob. If you want a legitimate way of showing off on a tennis court, one way to do it is by hitting this shot. It is used successfully by a small number of leading players, notably Tom Okker of the Netherlands. Most people's chances of pulling this shot off are about one in ten, but when it works, the applause is invariably deafening. And besides giving your ego a tremendous boost, it does really have its place. If your opponent is standing too close to the net, or if you just get a wild hair, then take a deep breath and have a little fun.

The topspin lob differs from both the defensive and the offensive lobs in that it is hit with tremendous topspin. The backswing is the same, but instead of just lifting the ball into the air, as you swing forward lower your racket and use your wrist and arm to bring the racket head sharply and violently up and over the top of the ball. Throw caution to the winds. In essence what you are hitting is a topspin forehand (or backhand) with a high trajectory, and if you execute the shot properly, once the ball reaches the peak of its line of flight (Line C) it will dive suddenly behind your opponent. It is very much an all-or-nothing shot. If you don't make an outright error, you will either hit an outright winner or hit the ball too short, in which case you'll soon have it stuffed back down your throat.

All other things being equal, hit a topspin lob crosscourt rather than down the line. The success or failure of this shot will be determined by the time the ball

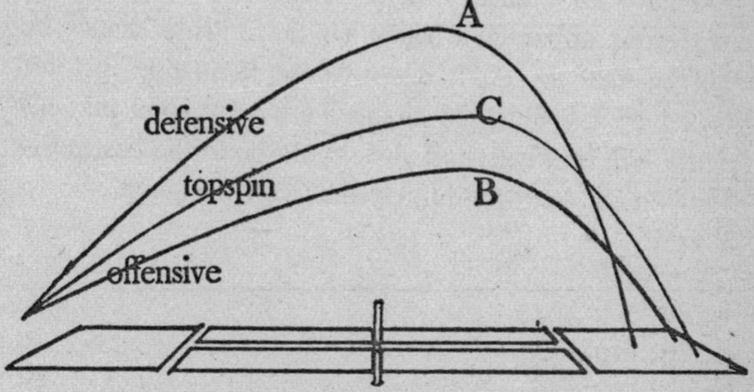

DIAGRAM 3/The trajectories of the offensive, defensive, and topspin lobs

reaches the point where your opponent is standing any-way, and what happens to the ball beyond that point is largely irrelevant—except that it must, of course, land safely in the court. And by hitting crosscourt you give yourself an extra three or four feet to work with.

Just to be on the safe side, always rush the net after you have hit a successful topspin lob (or any lob hit over your opponent's head) on the outside chance he will be able to run it down. Even if he does get his racket on the ball, the chances are very good that his return will be weak, and you should be in the best posi-tion—at the net—to quickly finish off the point.

The Half Volley

The half volley is a shot hit no more than one foot off the ground immediately after the ball bounces. It could just as well be called a half ground stroke, because it has as many characteristics of a forehand or backhand as it does of a volley. But whatever it's called, when you hit one it means one of two things: you really know your tennis or you're in deep trouble. It can be an at-tacking shot, and one player in particular, France's Henri Cochet, made a career out of the half volley in the 1920s and actually preferred it to a regular ground stroke. But he was an exception. Usually the half volley is hit in no man's land, just a few feet behind the service line, and means your opponent has hit a shot at your feet so that you have time neither to move forward an extra step and take the ball in the air nor retreat a few feet and hit it as a normal ground stroke. In other words, you've got problems and have to make the best of a bad situation.

When you see you're going to have to hit a half volley, immediately bend your knees and get down as low to the ground as you possibly can. Take very little backswing, if any at all. Hold the racket firmly parallel to the ground just behind where the ball is going to bounce. As you bring your racket forward, concentrate only on hitting the ball flat and making sure it makes solid contact with the racket. Place it as deep into your opponent's court as possible. Most of the time this will not be a powerful shot, and the best you can hope for is to hit deep enough so your opponent can't take control of the point. After you hit the shot, don't attempt to retreat but move forward quickly so you can regain the offensive with your next shot.

You'll find that you can't hit half volleys very hard, nor under most circumstances should you try. Just remember not to hurry your swing and that you're going to need an extra shot to extricate yourself from an awkward situation.

After the point is over, trace back the circumstances that made you have to hit a half volley in the first place. If your opponent hit a good shot and forced you into a defensive posture that's one thing, but most of the time you'll have to hit a half volley because of a miscalculation you made on the way to the net. Don't rush the net, either behind a service or a ground stroke, unless you're sure you can get there, and once you've decided to go forward don't change your mind halfway through the trip. This is an all too common fault, and the price you pay is having to hit the half volley.

The Drop Shot

The drop shot is one of the really fun shots of tennis.
If hit properly, it just barely clears the net and then
curls up on the ground and dies. And it's always worth
a round of applause, and more important, the drop shot
serves two strategic functions. It is a most effective way
to break the rhythm of your opponent's game (there is
nothing quite so disconcerting as to have to chase after
a dinky little drop shot when you've just hit two or three
great ground strokes), and it's a very good way to tire
your opponent. If you really have a bit of the sadist in
you, and a lot of touch, alternating drop shots and lobs
can be particularly devastating. Most players can run
all day from side to side, but very few men, and hardly
any women, can run up and back effectively.

A drop shot is hit with nearly the same swing as is
used for either the forehand or the backhand, except
that the backswing is a little shorter. Just before you
make contact with the ball lay your racket head back
and with a quick twist of your wrist hit sharply under
the ball. This will slow the ball down, and the pronounced underspin, or backspin, will eliminate much of
its forward bounce when it lands on your opponent's
side of the net. Don't hit the ball flat. You're liable
to hit it too hard, and if you do, it will probably
bounce forward just enough to let your opponent run
down the shot. The follow-through is short, but level, in
order to keep the ball's trajectory fairly flat.

Surprise is obviously of the essence. You should use
the shot only rarely, and never if you're standing on

your own base line. The ball will simply have to travel too far too slowly to be effective. Even the best drop shot can be run down if it's hit from that far away. Ideally, a drop shot should be hit at least halfway between your service line and the base line, and only when your opponent is on his base line.

The Drop Volley

The drop volley is just what its name implies, a drop shot hit from a volleying posture, and if it is properly executed it has exactly the same characteristics as a drop shot: the ball will just barely clear the net and die a sudden death when it lands on the other side. It requires a lot of touch.

To hit a drop volley, stick out your racket as though you were going to hit a normal volley. When the racket makes contact with the ball, don't attempt to follow through at all, but turn your wrist so the racket head comes under the ball and imparts a sharp backspin to it. Don't worry about power. Your aim is to let your racket absorb as much pace as it can and still get the ball back to the other side of the court. Nothing more.

Like a drop shot, the drop volley is fun to hit and has its place. But if you're in a position to hit a drop volley, you're also in a position to hit a normal volley, and one that will probably be a winner. Remember what I said earlier about not messing around when you have a chance to put away a shot. Hitting a drop volley is most definitely "messing around," and this shot should be tried no more than three or four times a match, or just enough to let your opponent know you can hit it.

The Lob Volley

The lob volley is the last individual shot to be considered, and with good reason. Of all the shots in your repertoire, this is the one that will be called upon least. The situations in which it can be used are very limited. The only times you will even be able to consider hitting it are during close-quarter volleying in doubles, or during those rare moments in a singles match when you and your opponent are eyeball to eyeball inside the service line. The lob volley can rarely be an outright winner, and its only purpose is as a convenient means to drive your opponent away from the net when you can't hit a normal, forceful volley.

To hit a lob volley, again just stick your racket out as though you were going to hit a normal volley, but as you bring your racket forward, use your whole arm and a stiff wrist to hit up on the ball and attempt to punch it over your opponent's head. Make sure you hit the ball firmly, even a little more firmly than you think necessary. If you hit a lob volley too short, you're going to be staring down the barrel of a gun—your opponent's overhead—and that is not a pleasant situation to be in at all. If the shot is well executed, fine. If it isn't—duck.

So there you have it. I have talked about all the shots, both the basic weapons and the added attractions, which comprise the complete tennis player's arsenal.

Obviously some shots are more important than others, which is why I talked about them in more depth. But the five covered in this chapter are important, too, and no player can aspire to greatness without the ability to hit all of them, even the ones he might use only once or twice during an afternoon's play.

Now that you have all the technical equipment, let's find out how it can best be used to produce winning tennis.

7 | Tennis to Win

Percentage Tennis

In this chapter, I'm assuming for the moment that you've done your homework well and fast and that you indeed have a well-balanced, all-round game without any glaring weaknesses. Now you are ready for some competitive tennis, and by that I mean you should have just one goal in mind when you walk on the court: to win the match by every legal and sporting means available to you. If your ultimate tennis objective is just to hit the ball around for a couple of hours and get some fresh air, then most of what I have to say from here to the end of the book won't have much meaning for you. What I want to talk about now are neither the nuances of the half volley nor the peculiarities of the forehand drive, but how to win. Nothing else.

Winning at tennis, just as with any other sport, demands a game plan. Such a plan is a compound of two basic elements. The first (which is what two-thirds of this chapter is about) is how you would play a match under ideal circumstances—in other words, what you would do if you had the perfect tennis game and your skills were the sole determinant of what went on during a match. The second element, which is imposed on these ideal court strategies, is a realistic allowance for the strengths and weaknesses of your game and that of your opponent. No matter how solid your game, some parts of it will be better than others, and some parts, although perhaps not weak, will be less strong. Likewise your opponent's game. From these two elements—one ideal, the other pragmatic—will come a very unemotional realization of what it is possible for you to do in certain situations, and this will be your overall court strategy.

Whatever you wind up with, the key to winning tennis is the ability to establish control of the match, and to do that you must be able to control more points than your opponent. Control is a very subjective matter, but it results from very objective things, and once a player develops a feel for the game it becomes as real and as tangible to him as the tennis balls or his racket. During a particular point you'll hit two or three shots and just *know* that you have the upper hand; even though you haven't hit the winning shot there is no question that the point is going to be yours. Suddenly, your opponent may break off just one great shot—not necessarily a winner—and now you know the balance of power has switched and you're the one who's on the defensive. I'm dramatizing a little bit, maybe, but to some degree this is what occurs on every single point and, on a bigger scale, in every game of every set and every set of every match. The ability to gain control (and to recognize that you have) is the primary key to successful tennis.

Percentage tennis, which can also be called "pattern tennis" or "position tennis," is nothing more than what you *should* do on a tennis court. Basically, it's a matter

of establishing head over heart. All players have pet
shots in which they like to indulge themselves, because
they are either spectacular or fun. Rosemary Casals
loves to hit a big running forehand volley, a really spectacular shot. But she is forever getting herself in trouble
because she can't hit it consistently. I love to hit drop
shots and drop volleys more than I should, and after a
while the surprise wears off, leaving the grandstands
clapping madly—for my opponent, who has just driven
the ball past me for a winner. The shots you like to hit
are often not the shots you should hit to best advance
your attack or improve your defensive position, whichever the case may be, and although you may get away
with these shots against inferior opponents, the chances
of their succeeding against players of your own ability
are slim, and against superior opponents, almost nonexistent.

Percentage tennis involves two things. First, it is hitting shots which have maximum effectiveness and, at
the same time, provide a comfortable margin of error.
Second, it is hitting shots which allow a player to position himself quickly and easily to cover his opponent's
return. A forcing shot that is not a winner is useless if
you allow your opponent to hit into an open court on
his return shot. The two things go very much together.

You should use these percentage shots 90 percent
of the time. Obviously you won't want to hit them all
of the time, because if you do you will play like a
computer programmed for just one task. That's like a
football team which has a good running attack but can't
throw the forward pass. If you hit ten forehands in a
row, in the same way and to the same part of the court,
even your dumbest opponent is going to catch on even-

tually. But if your opponent knows you can do three or four different things in a given situation, he's going to have to worry about all of them, and that obviously will increase the effectiveness of the shot you do hit the majority of the time.

But in general, hitting percentage shots is the most efficient and effective way to play tennis. After you finish this chapter, watch a match between two good professional players, men or women, and notice where they hit particular shots in certain situations. I think you'll slowly begin to see developing the patterns I'm going to talk about.

Just as you control a specific point by this method, so will you control the games, sets, and eventually the match. Pattern play is to tennis what a good outline is to a good essay. It's like ball control in football; it might take a football team an entire half to establish its superiority before it runs away with the game. The same thing holds true in tennis. If percentage tennis is employed properly, you, hopefully, will be able to feel the entire momentum of the match slowly turn in your favor, even though the score for a time might remain close. So be patient. The only point that counts is the last one.

During every match you ever play you will be doing one of three things. You will be rushing the net, or defending against a net rusher, or, if neither you nor your opponent has any desire to take the net, you will be playing the backcourt game. To fill in this sketchy outline with all the subtle strategic possibilities would, of course, take an encyclopedia, but, essentially, tennis does boil down to a consideration of these three general situations.

Rushing the Net

There are two ways to get to the net, either behind a service or behind a strong forcing ground stroke, and the first way is the one you will obviously use the most. Let's consider the extreme possibilities of just one point as seen by someone with a healthy serve-and-volley game who is serving from the deuce court, and see how percentage tennis comes into play. The first consideration, of course, is getting to the net. In the chapter on the service I emphasized that success depends to a large degree on hitting the serve with a good, uninterrupted rhythm. There are two reasons for this. First, good rhythm helps you time the service itself, and second, the same forward motion that supplies a part of the power to the service also gives you a good start toward the net. The distance between the base line and your service line is eighteen feet. From the time you hit your service to the time your opponent hits his return, you should be able to cover at least fifteen of those feet and come to a complete stop in the position where you can best cover the two extreme lines of flight that the return of service can follow. The two most common errors in this regard are failing to come in far enough and failing to halt your forward movement by the time your opponent hits the ball. In the first case you will find yourself hung up in no man's land, and in the second you are likely to be caught moving toward one side of the court when the ball is headed toward the other. Avoid them both.

All right. Now, one of the objectives of every shot is

to leave yourself with as little court as you possibly
can to cover on your opponent's return. In the deuce
court, you can serve either right down the middle or to
the extreme right-hand corner of your opponent's service
court. (Or anywhere in between, of course. But keep
in mind that I'm talking about extreme cases.) In Diagram 4 these two possibilities are indicated by broken
lines. If you serve down the middle, your opponent
will hit the ball from position X, and his two extreme
return possibilities are along the lines XC and XD. If
his return is any more angled than either of these, roll
up your eyeballs and give him credit for a great shot. If
it's hit any deeper to either your forehand or your backhand side, the angle CXD decreases, which—remember
your plane geometry—works to your advantage. So in
this particular situation you have twenty-seven feet, the
width of the court, to worry about covering.

But now consider the wide service to your opponent's
position Z. One possible extreme return is still to point
C on your side of the court, but the other is not merely
to point D, as might seem the case, but to point T,
which is about halfway between your service line and
the net. The reason for allowing this more sharply
angled return is simple: it can be hit with a margin of
error that is every bit as great as the ZC return. Here's
why. This shot—the crosscourt return—as shown in
this diagram is only three feet shorter in length than
the down-the-line return, line ZC. This means it can
be hit nearly as hard as the down-the-line return and
still land safely. Also, remember that the net is highest
at the sidelines and tapers gradually to its low point in
the center of the court, so the ZT return actually crosses
a lower part of the net than does the ZC, which means

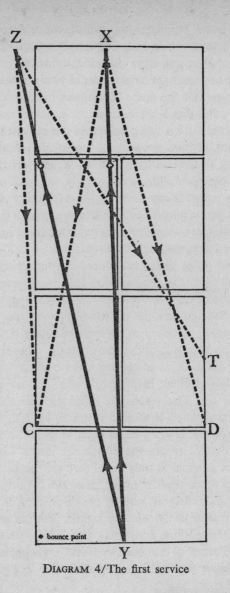

DIAGRAM 4/The first service

that the ZT can be hit even harder. Obviously a shot along ZD would be a little bit safer than one long ZT. But what your opponent loses by hitting a shot with a slightly smaller margin of error he more than makes up by greatly increasing his angle of return. Draw in the line ZD and see for yourself.

This is the angle of return I mentioned in passing earlier in the book. Here's why it's so important. If you hit a wide serve you no longer have just twenty-seven feet to worry about covering, but nearly thirty feet—the length of the imaginary line CT. Giving your opponent the chance to hit that sharply angled return along ZT is what makes the difference, and if he hits his return hard, that difference will be accentuated even more. The obvious conclusion is to hit your service, at least the first one, down the middle. Look again at the paths of your two possible services, and note that the one down the middle passes over the low part of the net very nearly right at the center of the court, but the one wide to your opponent's forehand passes over the net about halfway to your left sideline. That extra three inches or so is also working against you.

Now let's continue to play this imaginary point in Diagram 5. Let's presume that you indeed have served down the middle and that the return of service has been hit fairly sharply to your backhand side. You have moved from your first ready position, P_0 (which you took while you waited to see where your opponent's return was going), and are now ready to hit your first volley from position P_1, just inside the service line. The general rule in percentage tennis is always to hit your first volley down the line when you cannot hit a winner and always to volley crosscourt when you do go for a winner. Here are the reasons.

From P_1 you have two options. You can hit the volley either down the line to B or crosscourt to A. Consider the alternatives. If you hit down the line to B, your opponent's possible second shots are along the lines BC and BT (BT rather than BD for the same reasons I favored ZT over ZD while just discussing Diagram 4), and remembering what I said in an earlier chapter about always moving toward the net after each shot, you would probably take up a position at P_2 after your first volley, then stop and wait to see where your opponent hit his second shot. Your movement from P_1 to P_2 would be a nice, straight-line forward progression, during which you could keep your left sideline well covered. The left sideline needs more protection because a down-the-line return will reach you sooner than a crosscourt return hit at the same speed. This is because the crosscourt return has farther to travel. If the return did come back crosscourt along BT, then the steps you would take to cover that shot would still be slightly forward toward the net.

The alternative is to hit your first volley crosscourt to point A. But now, in order to protect against the possibility of a down-the-line second shot by your opponent, along the line AD, you would have to move to P_3. However, this not only involves more steps but requires more of a sideways movement than a forward one. This may seem like a minor point, but when you move from P_1 to P_3, which you must do, and if your opponent chooses to hit his second shot crosscourt along the line AR, you have much more to worry about than just covering a plain crosscourt. Your opponent then

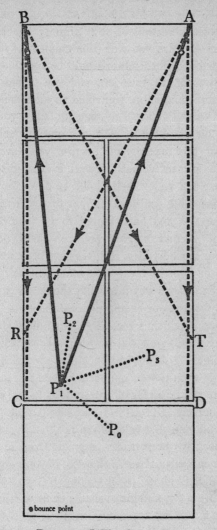

DIAGRAM 5/The first volley

will have come up with the classic winning shot in tennis, which is a ball hit behind you—that is, one hit in the opposite direction of your primary line of movement. In this case you would be moving to your right and your opponent's return would be traveling against this movement, to your left, and you would have to change direction before you could go after the ball and hit your second volley. Any time you allow your opponent to hit this kind of shot, you put yourself in the hole. For this reason, and because you have to run farther to protect yourself against a down-the-line return, your first volley itself should be down the line.

So, presuming you have hit your first volley properly down the line and have moved to P_2 to await your opponent's second shot, let's consider where you should place your second volley. If things have been going well, this will be your putaway volley and will be hit crosscourt. The reasons why this volley should go crosscourt, whereas the first one should not, are shown in Diagram 6. If your opponent's second shot is indeed down the line (along BC) you will hit your second volley from P_5 to point S. You will be hitting into a practically open court, and even if your opponent should run down this volley, he will be so far off the court as to make a good return unlikely. But if you had hit to that position, point S, on your first volley from position P_1, the angle would not have been nearly as great. Draw in the line P_1S for yourself and see. Likewise, if your opponent's second shot is hit crosscourt along BT, you will take the shot from P_4, and the available angle will be almost as great if you hit crosscourt to point Q. But if you had hit to Q from P_1, the flight of the ball would have

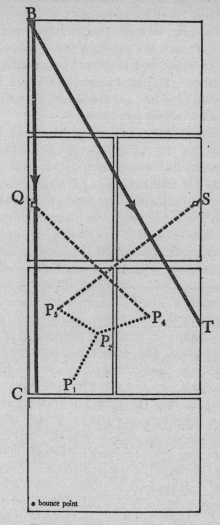

DIAGRAM 6/The putaway volley

taken it almost directly back to where it came from, and you would have gained nothing.

In either case, the more sharply angled your volley, the better chance it has of being a winner, and you can't hit sharply angled volleys unless you are close to the net. Under normal circumstances you won't be close to the net when you hit your first volley, but you should be by the time you hit your second.

The same principles hold true if you consider a rush to the net from the backcourt, as shown in Diagram 7. Let's presume that from position P_0 you have gotten a nice, short ball and have decided to take the net. Again you have the choice of hitting crosscourt to point B or down the line to point A. If you hit crosscourt you will have to move forward to P_2 to cover your opponent's two return possibilities, which are down the line along BC or crosscourt along BT. If you hit down the line, your opponent can return along AD or AR and your ready position will be P_1. Regardless of where you hit your approach shot, to B or A, you will have to cover the same amount of ground to protect against his return possibilities. That doesn't change. But by hitting crosscourt you create the same problems you would have created if your first volley had gone crosscourt in the earlier example (Diagram 5). Your primary consideration is the same—to protect yourself against the down-the-line return. And if you hit your approach down the line, your opponent's down-the-line return is covered during all of the time you are advancing to P_1. But if your approach is crosscourt, your opponent's down-the-line return is now along your left sideline, which is uncovered until you actually reach P_2. Further, the line from P_0 to P_2 is longer than the line from

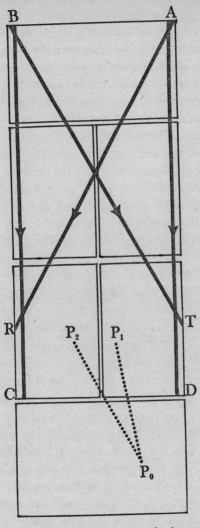

DIAGRAM 7/The approach shot

P_0 to P_1, which means you have more ground to cover. And finally, your opponent's crosscourt return—along BT—will be hit behind you (against the direction of your advance), while a crosscourt hit from A would be in the same direction as your line of advance. On all three counts the down-the-line approach shot is best.

That, essentially, is it—from the net rusher's point of view. The diagrams and the situations are oversimplified, of course, and do not take into account the many varieties of play and subtle options available to both you and your opponent. I have not talked about the many different kinds of spins, speeds, court surfaces, and the like, all of which are considerations, and very important ones, when you plan your shots. And it may seem that the differences which have dictated what I said to do are minuscule. After all, three or four extra feet really isn't a lot of ground to cover. But consider a couple of things. First, in these diagrams the court appears long and narrow, and it looks as though it would be fairly easy to cover any shot hit almost anywhere. But believe me, against a hard-hitting opponent who knows his tennis, that court can appear as wide as a football field. And second, presuming you're a fairly fast reader and that your geometry's in good shape, it may have taken you eight or ten minutes to read this far into this chapter. But the actual time it would take to play the two partial points I have described is something like ten seconds. That really doesn't give you a whole lot of time to think about all the options available to you on a given point, and if you can decide in advance what shots work the best you will have freed your mind to concentrate on the execution of the shots themselves.

Defending Against the Net Rusher

Trade places with your opponent. Now he is the one rushing the net, and whether the rush comes behind a service or a ground stroke, you are essentially in a defensive posture and must wage a sort of guerrilla warfare until you can counterattack and gain the net for yourself. But even though you are on the defensive, there are a few things you can do to neutralize his advantage, or at the very least make it more difficult for him to pursue his attack. Just as you use percentage tennis when you rush the net, so can you use it when you defend against a net rusher. In general, you can pursue one of two strategies: either you can try to hit the ball past your opponent and hope that your passing shots are better than his volleys, or you can ignore potentially winning shots and just keep the ball in play and hope you will force a weak return.

If you pursue the first strategy, the question is whether you should hit down the line or crosscourt, and the answer is the same now as it was when you were rushing the net—don't hit crosscourt unless you're almost positive your shot will be a winner, or will force a weak return. There are two reasons for this. First, in the diagrams I just reviewed I indicated that a ball hit down the line by the receiver is going to reach the net rusher more quickly than one hit crosscourt, simply because the crosscourt has farther to travel. This is why the net rusher must protect himself primarily against the down-the-line return, and this is also why your most effective return is down the line. Second, if a crosscourt return is weak, your opponent will have almost the entire court to hit into. If you hit a return down the line, you automatically have half the court covered—the half your opponent will hit into if he hits his return volley back down the line (which, as I said earlier, should be his preference). But if your shot goes crosscourt, you must think about protecting your far sideline, too, and this means running hard to a position at least equidistant between the two sidelines. Now your opponent can do two things with the ball, either of which could make trouble for you. He can volley down the line to your backhand, which means you will have to run from one side of the court to the other in order to get to the ball, or he can volley crosscourt, which means he will have hit the ball in the direction opposite the one you're running—behind you. And you don't want to have to change directions quickly in the backcourt any more than you do at the net.

In general, the more your opponent crowds the net, the more you will want to hit returns down the line. The farther back your opponent is, the better angle of return you can get on crosscourt shots, but they should still be hit only when you're pretty sure of coming through with a winner, or, at the very least, of forcing a weak return.

The second basic strategy—hitting soft shots at the net rusher's feet instead of going for outright winners—I talked about in some detail in Chapter 2 in connection with the return of service, and I won't repeat myself now. Let me just warn that this kind of shot should be used only when your opponent is on the way up to the net. Its object is to force your opponent to hit up on the ball, but if he's already at the net, he can pounce on a softly hit ball while it's still above the level of the net and put it away without much difficulty at all.

Let me make two final points, both of which are pretty obvious but occasionally overlooked:

First, take another look at the diagrams in the preceding section. In all of them the defender's returns are hit short. None is diagrammed to land any deeper than the net rusher's service line. When your opponent rushes the net you don't have to hit a deep shot—one that kicks up chalk on the base line—to get the ball past him. He has already taken care of the depth problem by coming forward. Use this to your advantage. You can get more of an angle on a short shot than you can on a deep one, and angles are what you are after, not only when you rush the net but when you are defending against the net rusher as well.

Second, if you succeed in forcing a weak or short volley from your opponent, pounce on it immediately and move toward the net. It's nice to neutralize your opponent's initial advantage (and important), but it doesn't mean a thing unless you take advantage of it and get to the net yourself.

Playing the Backcourt Game

I firmly believe that today the best approach for a young player who hopes to achieve world-class standing is an all-round game with an emphasis on a strong serve and volley. The lack of the Big Game is a hindrance but not an insurmountable obstacle for a player who aspires to greatness, as many players over the years have proved. Among women, Ann Jones is the best example of a backcourt player who has reached the top. Nearly all the modern European male players, who learn to play on a very slow clay, are proponents of the backcourt game, foremost among them Manuel Santana of Spain. And in the United States, Bitsy Grant in the 1930s, Bobby Riggs in the 1940s, Bernard "Tut" Bartzen in the 1950s, and Cliff Richey in the 1960s more than held their own against the great net rushers of their day. But even if you never play on clay in your life, you still need solid ground strokes and should be aware of backcourt strategic considerations to reach tennis maturity. Besides, playing from the base line is in some ways more challenging and more fun and requires more intelligence than the Big Game. There is nothing more enjoyable than watching a good base-liner challenge a good net rusher, or a battle between two base-liners who know what they're doing. In matches like these, tennis takes on the dimensions of a high-speed game of chess.

So if you are one of those players who is physically and/or temperamentally more suited to the backcourt game, then by all means pursue it.

A base-liner wins points in one of two ways. Either he forces errors by his opponents, or he forces such weak returns that he will be able to hit winning shots from the backcourt—or even from the net on occasion. Let me emphasize that by a backcourt game I am not talking about merely playing the kind of steady game in which two players stand on the base line, hit semi-lobs at each other, and wait interminably for somebody to make an error. This is not tennis, it is just patballing or dinking. And whatever you choose to call it, it is generally accompanied by a great deal of the running around of weaknesses and the avoidance of attacking shots. It surely does nothing to improve a player's tennis game; on the contrary, it hinders the development of solid ground strokes, and, after a while, generally results in nothing but so much frustration and boredom. You don't sign a nonaggression pact when you choose to play from the base line. No. The shots in the backcourt game I am talking about are, in their own way, as carefully calculated and as aggressively executed as the hardest services and the most sharply angled volley.

If you play from the backcourt, you should hit every shot with three goals in mind. The first is to keep your opponent away from the net. Like you, your opponent probably will play on the base line only because his volley is average, not because it is nonexistent. If your ground strokes are sufficiently shallow and weak, even a mediocre volleyer will rush the net and hit winning volleys against you. Make sure all of your shots have enough depth and pace to keep the other player in the backcourt. The second goal is to make your opponent work hard for everything, and this means running him as much as you can. The third goal is to hit each shot with increasingly more angle so that eventually your opponent is drawn off the court enough for you to hit an outright winner, or at least to force him into an error.

To accomplish all of this you will use two basic patterns. The first is a series of shots hit from one sideline to the other. When you have the time to get perfectly set, you should always attempt to hit your shots as far away from your opponent as possible. You don't

necessarily have to hit the ball hard every time, but
make sure he has to cover plenty of ground between
each shot. You won't tire anybody out by hitting balls
right down the middle, nor will you find yourself with
an open court to hit into after three or four shots. And
you will frustrate yourself and your strategy if, for example, you hit a shot wide to your opponent's forehand,
follow it up with a shot wide to his backhand and then,
when he's really on a string, let him go by placing the
third shot in an eminently reachable position right back
up the middle. After a couple of wide shots in a row, if
they are well executed, you should be able to take a
gamble and really slug one for a winner. If your opponent, say, has just hit a shot from very wide on his
backhand side, your winning shot can be either wide
and deep to his forehand, or short and hard back to
his backhand side. Again, with the latter shot you will
have hit behind your opponent and forced him to change
directions rapidly before he can set himself, and when
successful, this almost always produces a weak return,
if any at all.

The second pattern is a series of shots hit alternately
deep and short. I'm not now necessarily talking about
the drop shot and lob strategy I mentioned earlier, but
one in which you first hit a short, angled shot, usually
crosscourt, to one side of your opponent's court, then
hit the following one deep to the opposite corner, and
repeat as many times as necessary. Women especially
cannot run up and back nearly as well as they can run
from side to side, and it's difficult for anyone caught
in this pattern to break out of it. Of course, if your opponent doesn't like to play at the net in the first place,
then by all means do everything in your power to make

sure he spends a lot of time there, even to the point of hitting purposely bad drop shots so he has to come up. If he takes the net, you've got him right where he doesn't want to be, and if he attempts to scurry back to the base line, your next shot will probably catch him in no man's land, where almost any kind of decent shot will be a winner.

As you plan and execute your shots you should always do the following three things:

Give yourself a solid margin of error. More than likely you will not attempt to hit an outright winner until the fourth or fifth shot of a point, and pinpoint accuracy and tremendous pace simply aren't necessary. On a passing shot you generally have to hit the ball hard and usually have to go for the line in order to get your shot past the player at the net, but when your opponent is in the backcourt you have much greater leeway. If your shots are hit with medium pace and land anywhere around six or eight feet from your opponent's sideline or base line, you will have accomplished your purpose. Remember that you are not trying to win the point with one shot.

Keep your patience. You may hit two or three well-placed, angled ground strokes and think your opponent is really on the hook, only to have him suddenly extricate himself with a really great shot that will stop your momentum or perhaps even put you on the defensive. In a case like this, all you can do is shrug your shoulders and retreat. Remember, your opponent is trying to do the same things you are, so give credit where it's due and then start in all over again. It takes longer to win a point from the base line than it does from the net, so keep your cool.

Put a lot of spin on the ball and hit a lot of cross-courts. Pace is not of primary importance, and the more spin you put on the ball—either topspin or underspin—the easier it will be to control your shots. Remember, too, that the net is six inches lower in the middle than it is at the sidelines and that a crosscourt shot passes over the lowest part of the net, demands less accuracy than a down-the-line and can travel up to five feet farther than a down-the-line and still land safely in your opponent's court. So until you get the shot with which you can begin one of the patterns I talked about earlier, hit crosscourts. They're safer and easier to execute, and unless you rely too heavily on them, their extensive use won't affect your backcourt strategies in the least.

Some Case Histories

Obviously, what I have just presented, in the discussion of both the serve-and-volley game and the backcourt game, is nothing more than the bare framework for what actually will happen on a tennis court. Unless your opponent is a simpleton, in which case there won't be any problem in the first place, you aren't going to be able to "run the same play," as it were, on every point. Every volley you hit is not going to have the perfect crispness, nor every ground stroke the perfect depth and pace, to allow you to force the point as you might wish. And then there is always your opponent to consider. What happens during a match depends ultimately more on your strengths and weaknesses and on those of your opponent than on any textbook presentation of the ideal way to play a match. The strong parts of your game will take care of themselves; the weak ones must be compensated for. In the case of your opponent, you must be aware of what he does best and at the same time be ready to exploit his weaknesses.

Your game and that of your opponent should first be analyzed on very basic grounds. Do you have an unreliable backhand? If so, perhaps you should avoid the shot whenever you can do so without getting yourself out of position too much (remember that I'm talking about playing to win now), or perhaps you should lob a little more from that side. Is your volley weak? Then don't rush the net as often as you might like. Wait for a perfect shot to come in behind. Do you have a superb overhead? Then you can get away with crowding the net and perhaps even tease your opponent into lobbing more than he otherwise might. And there are the smaller considerations. Does your opponent always hit his forehand crosscourt? If so, play a little more to your right side and invite him to attempt a forehand down the line. Does his first service land a little short? Then move in a step or two on your return of service and attempt to take the initiative away from him immediately. Does he have trouble moving backward and to his left? Then be sure and lob to his backhand side.

If you earnestly analyze your own game and that of your opponent, eventually you will be able to pit your strengths against his weaknesses. And eventually, too, this sort of dissection will become almost second nature, and you'll be able to make proper adjustments in your court strategy even as a match is in progress. Your opponent might miss five overheads in a row at the beginning of the afternoon and then not miss one the rest of the day. If you train yourself to notice such things (and in this case stop lobbing him), winning will become much simpler for you.

I obviously don't know your game personally, nor those of your possible opponents, and so I won't presume to offer any specific advice. But what I would like to do is take three sample situations from my own experience that may suggest how you should approach match-play situations of your own.

1. Virginia Wade is the British player who won the first United States Open singles championship at Forest Hills, New York, in 1968. She has a very steady backhand and a very powerful but (at least so far) erratic forehand. Logic would seem to dictate that I play her forehand. But in a crucial situation—if, for example, it's 30–40 and I need to win the point or else lose my service—I invariably serve to her backhand. Here's why. It's true that her forehand is more erratic than her backhand, but she also whales away at the forehand with tremendous confidence, and if I serve to that side, one of two things will happen. She will either make a wild error, which is nice, or she will hit the ball past me for a winner, because I won't have the foggiest notion where's she's going to hit the ball. On the other hand, if I hit to her backhand, she most always will get the ball back in play, but with less pace, and I'll have plenty of time to figure out where her return will come. Therefore, I'll sacrifice the chance to win the point on one shot for the burden of hitting a service and one or two volleys, but in the long run, simply because I have a better chance of knowing where she is going to place

that return of service, the percentages will be on my side.

2. I said earlier in this chapter that the most logical shot against a good net rusher is a down-the-line return, but Maria Bueno, the graceful Brazilian player, presents a special problem. When she rushes the net, and even after she hits her first volley, she has a tendency to hang back on the service line. Therefore I cannot lob her, because from that position even a perfect lob is an easy shot for her. But remember that when a net rusher hangs back, he leaves himself open for the crosscourt, which is an easier shot to hit anyway. So that's exactly the shot I'll hit. But although Maria hangs back, she will occasionally rush to the net very quickly—generally when I least expect it—and that's what I have to watch out for. When she does that, a lob is the only shot I can hit because by then she will be right on top of the net and can easily put away all but the best passing shots.

3. Margaret Smith Court, the Australian who won more major titles during the 1960s than any other player, presents the opportunity for a slightly different approach against a topnotch net rusher. Margaret is very tall and really quite intimidating when she hits one of her big services and comes storming to the net. Most kids who play her for the first time panic a little bit and think they have to hit a winner right away or the point's all over. That's the way I felt the first few times I played her, but I soon found out what worked better. Instead of going for a passing shot, I'll just hit that little soft, sliced return I have been talking about right at her feet, just as slow and low as I can get it. Margaret al-

ways uses her strength to great advantage, and my job is to see that she doesn't get the opportunity to use that power. The slower my returns are, the more difficult it is for her—or for anybody—to hit the ball hard in return. Then on the very next shot, that's when I'll go for my winner. I'll take a couple of steps into the court, and maybe even try to volley my second shot. I am quicker and more flexible than she is, and this mobility is what I can use to offset her greater strength.

These three examples briefly show the way you should be thinking and what you should watch for during, and in anticipation of, every match you play. For any one opponent, the specific considerations will be different, but the thinking process will be the same. First decide what you *should* do, then analyze yourself and your opponent. Finally, put the two together and plan what it is *possible* for you to do during the match. And then, the best of luck.

Know the Score

A peripheral strategic consideration arises from the fact that tennis, for reasons of history which I won't go into, has an unusual scoring system. In fact, it's downright weird. In baseball, every time you cross home plate, that's a run and it counts one. In football, a touchdown counts six, an extra point one, a field goal three, and a safety two. At the end of the game you add everything up and see whether you have a higher total than your opponent. Tennis, of course, is different. You win points

in order to win games, games in order to win sets, and
sets in order to win matches, and it is quite possible
for you to win more points than your opponent and still
lose the match. When Rod Laver took the 1969 United
States Open singles title he won seven matches and lost
none, but still won only 54.4 percent of the points he
played. (A few experimental scoring systems have been
tried during the past few years in an effort to straighten
all of this out, but the chances are that none will come
into widespread use, at least not in the near future.)
The result is that some points are strategically and psy-
chologically—but not actually—worth more than others.
This is not to say you shouldn't bear down on every
point, and in every game and set—you always read or
hear about some player who has either blown a big lead
or rallied to win from the brink of defeat—but merely
that there are situations in a match which have more
effect on the outcome than others. You should know
what these situations are and play accordingly.

These situations are accentuated when you and your
opponent are both playing the Big Game and are fairly
even in ability. In a match like this, a set is usually determined by just one service break, and your overriding
strategic goal is to hold your service and break your
opponent's. If you and your opponent both play from
the base line, breaking service is less of a deciding
factor, but in either case there are still certain key
situations.

The fourth point is considered by many players the
pivotal one of each game. Consider the possibilities. If
you are ahead 40–love or trailing love–40, the situation
is obvious. In the first instance if you win the fourth
point the game is yours. In the second, you need to win

the point to stay in the game. No problem there. But consider when you are serving at 30–15. Now the fourth point ceases to be just another point, but one upon which the entire game turns. If you win this point, you are ahead 40–15 and your opponent must win two straight points just to pull even with you. If you lose the point, the score is 30–30, and instead of the odds being overwhelmingly in your favor they are now only slightly so. (It is fair to assume a slight statistical advantage in favor of the server on every point.) If you serve at 15–30 and lose the point, your opponent then has two straight chances to break your service and the odds that he will are strongly in his favor. But if you win that point you're back to 30–30 and on your way to reestablishing control of the game.

If you are receiving service, everything is reversed. If you trail by 30–15 and lose the fourth point, you're probably going to lose that game; if you win it, it's a tie ballgame. If you're ahead by 15–30, winning the fourth point gives you two straight chances to break service, but if you lose the point you have allowed the server to reassume control.

What it all boils down to is this: the first three points of a game should be played fairly straight. Do the things you would normally do and don't be upset if you lose a point or two, or be overly exhilarated if you win a point or two. A 30–love or 30–15 lead is nice, but not conclusive, nor is a 0–30 or 15–30 deficit cause for great anguish. But the points that can bring you to game point or keep your opponent from reaching game point are the crucial ones, and should be considered as such. This is when you reach down a little deeper, concentrate a little harder, and fight a little more tenaciously. Obviously, the deuce and advantage points have nearly the same importance as that fourth point, but the really big moments are those when you have a chance to take conclusive control of a game, or when you desperately need a point to stay in contention. This is when you find out what kind of nerves and skills you really have.

By the same token, the key games of a set are the seventh and eighth, and it is during these two games that either your superiority or your opponent's is most likely to show itself. Of course, after six games the set could be over, or you could be ahead by 5–1 or trail by 1–5, in which cases the pattern of the set would be obvious. But if after the initial parry and thrust of the first six games—during which you and your opponent each will have served three times—you and your opponent are still pretty even, the time will have come to assert yourself. There are three possibilities.

If you lead by four games to two, it means you have already achieved a service break. Wonderful. If you hold that margin through two more games, you'll be up 5–3 and within a game of the set. If you lose your service in either of these games (which one, of course, depends on whether you are serving the odd or even games), your opponent will have drawn even and will probably have the momentum on his side.

If you trail by 2–4, everything is reversed. If you don't break service quickly your opponent will be on the brink of winning the set; if you do break his serve, you'll have pulled even and turned the tide in your favor.

If the score is 3–3 and you break service, you will be at 5–3 again (presuming you hold your own), but if your opponent breaks you, he will have the 5–3 edge.

In all three cases, a matter of a service break in the seventh or eighth game brings the player who achieves it to within a game of the set—and possibly puts him over the top. The games that bring you this close to victory, or defeat, are the ones in which to bear down, just as you should bear down on the point that brings you nearest to winning a game.

Similarly, on a larger scale the second set of a best-of-three match (and the third set of a best-of-five) is the most crucial. Obviously, if you win the opening set and follow up by winning the second, the match is over. But if you win the first and lose the second, your opponent can feel pretty secure in the knowledge that the match's momentum has switched to him. And conversely, if you lose the first set but rally to win the second, you can justifiably say to yourself that the first set was a fluke and that you really are in control. So don't let up if you win the first set of a match, and don't become too discouraged if you lose it. The player who wins the second one stands the best chance of winning the match.

Momentum, whether within a point, game, set, or match, is an intangible thing, but very real, and to sense that it's on your side is a great plus.

The last strategic consideration I would like to mention involves changing a losing style of play. It may seem obvious that if your original game plan is not working you should try something else. But it's not quite that simple, because despite what the scoreboard says it is sometimes quite difficult to decide if indeed you are losing—at least if you are losing decisively—or why.

The time for this soul searching is about midway through the second set (of a best-of-three match). If you lost the first set by only a service break and trail in the second by just a couple of games, say 1–3 or 2–4, then you are faced with a difficult decision. If you have worked out a proper court strategy you are undoubtedly playing the type of game that you are most comfortable with and that allows you to play your best tennis. Did you lose the first set by a hair? Do you trail now only because one or two points went the wrong way? If so, then stick to your guns and hope that eventually a couple of key points will fall your way and permit you to get back into the match.

But if you lost the first set decisively and your service has already been broken at least once in the second, then you should probably give up your original plan and try something—anything—different. If you started out by playing the Big Game, then keep away from the net and hit everything from the base line. If you first tried to beat your opponent from the backcourt, then start rushing the net. Even though your new strategy won't be "your" game, if you continue to play the way you started out you're going to lose anyway, and you have absolutely nothing to lose by trying something different. It's a tough decision to make, but many players become so enamored of their favorite style of play that they simply refuse to face reality and, in effect, commit tennis suicide. It's all very noble to stick to your guns, but not if your gunpowder is wet that particular day. And who knows? By merely changing your style you might so shake up your opponent that he will falter for a few games and allow you to pull even. Or it might help you cut down on your own mistakes. Either way, you're in better shape than you were before, and surely no worse off.

8 | The Doubles Game

It would take another entire book—I would recommend Billy Talbert and Bruce Olds' *The Game of Doubles in Tennis* (Lippincott, 1968, 3rd edition)—to explain all the subtleties of doubles strategy and shotmaking. Over the years there have been several players who, although they have not been able to reach the ranks of the world's best in singles, have gained esteemed and legitimate reputations on the doubles court. Because the demands of doubles are different, it does not necessarily follow that two superb singles players will make a good doubles team. Above all else, doubles requires teamwork, and a singles player just simply might be incapable of subverting his natural individualistic tendencies to the good of the team. But for those of you who do like to play doubles, let me make a few points that may suggest what this tantalizing and interesting subset of tennis is all about.

1. When you are picking a partner, first and foremost seek out a player you can live with. You don't have to be bosom buddies, but you at least have to respect each other's abilities. Tennis, as I have suggested, is not so

much a game of placements as it is of errors, and during the course of a match you and your partner are both going to make your fair share. In singles, there is nobody to blame but yourself when things don't go right. But in doubles you're occasionally going to have to fight the urge to blame your partner for all the misfortune you might encounter. If you respect his ability from the beginning, and he respects yours, you will eliminate a lot of nasty intramural bickering.

2. The ideal doubles team is composed of one player with great strength—a superior service, a punishing overhead, and so forth—and one who, although unable to hit the ball very hard, rarely makes an error. On a team like this—or even on a team where the players' styles are not quite so contrasted—the steadier doubles player should play the advantage court, because that is where most of the crucial points are played.

3. The overwhelming majority of doubles points are decided at the net. You can lose points from the backcourt but you can rarely win them from there. Thus your primary objective is *always* to rush the net, even in what would otherwise be borderline situations, and if your opponents are already there, to force them away from it. The doubles court is only nine feet wider than the singles court, and when your opponents are properly positioned at the net it is almost impossible to hit a ground stroke past both of them. Defensive tennis has its place in singles but rarely in doubles. So make the taking of that net your primary objective, and only retreat from it in an emergency.

4. Position is more important than power. You can rarely win a point outright with just one or two shots. Therefore, every shot should be hit primarily with the thought of improving your position—that is, getting closer to the net—so that eventually you will be able to force a weak return and end the point with a volley or overhead.

5. Now look at Diagram 8. You are serving from position A, your partner is at the net in position B, and your opponents are at C and D awaiting your service into the deuce court. Your partner's primary objective is to cover his left sideline and force your opponent to hit his return crosscourt. Therefore he will position himself about halfway between his left sideline and the center of the court. As you serve and rush the net, you must cover the other half of your court, and to do this best the rule is exactly the same as in singles—serve down the middle. If you serve to the outside (and this applies to the advantage court as well), you allow your opponent to hit a more sharply angled return, which means more court for you to cover. Also, since your primary objective is to get to the net, hit your service, both the first and the second, with more topspin and less pace than you would in singles. This gives you greater insurance that your service will go in and also allows you more time to rush the net. In singles your first volley is hit from right at the service line; in doubles it should be hit from well inside the service line. And since you don't want to hit to the opponents' netman any more than they want to hit to yours, your first volley should be hit low, either down the middle or crosscourt.

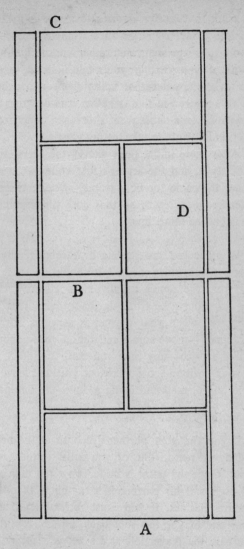

DIAGRAM 8/The ready positions for doubles

6. When you receive service, your goal is to force a weak first volley. Don't go for a winner; your chances of hitting one are slim. But rather hit the ball slower and with more angle than you might normally use, and try to make the net rusher volley from below the net. Once you succeed in that, whether it is on your return of service or on a subsequent shot, then come forward quickly and attempt to take the net yourself.

7. After these initial three shots—the serve, the return of serve, and the server's first volley—the objectives are the same for both teams, namely, to force a sufficiently weak return so that both partners can be at the net at the same time.

8. Whether you are serving or receiving, any time the netman can volley the ball he should do so. A good volley from the net is usually more effective than a strong ground stroke from the backcourt. This is especially true when your partner is serving. Then you should poach—move across and cut off your opponent's return of service—any time you can. But don't move from your position too quickly, or you will leave your sideline unprotected and invite a down-the-line passing shot.

9. If you and your partner are both at the net and for whatever reason one of you must retreat, retreat together. Once the point is under way, the man at the net is useless if his partner is scrambling all over the backcourt. Besides, if you must retreat, it is usually because one of you has sent back a weak return, and in that case the player left at the net is a sitting duck. Likewise, rush the net together once you can regain the

attack. A team with one player up and another player back is a team in trouble.

10. The lob is an extremely effective weapon in doubles play. Since there are two of you covering one side of the court, a good lob is extremely difficult for your opponents to put away, and is often the only shot that can force a well-entrenched team back from the net.

11. Teamwork is of the essence, in two situations in particular. First, when a ball is hit down the middle between you and your partner, for gosh sakes make sure somebody swings at it. Far too many points are lost because each partner thinks the other is going to take a ball hit equidistant between them. Ideally, you and your partner should reach some sort of agreement beforehand on how to handle shots between you. But if there is ever any doubt go for the ball yourself. It's better occasionally to clash rackets (which doesn't happen very often anyway) than to let a ball that both of you could have reached land between you for a winner. Second, when your partner can't judge whether his ball is going to land in or out, give him some help. In the heat of a fast exchange it's natural to swing at everything within range, but if it's obvious to you that your partner is about to hit an out ball, don't hesitate to tell him about it. And don't whisper; shout.

9 | Practice and Other Annoyances

Good tennis is basically a matter of knowing how to hit a variety of shots and when and where to hit them. But there are other considerations, too, which have a direct bearing on your performance. The most important of these are how well you practice; what kind of shape you keep yourself in; your knowledge of how various court surfaces can affect your play; how effectively you counter the sometimes annoying outside elements, especially wind, sun, and heat, and make them work to your advantage; and finally, how you conduct yourself on the court during a match.

How to Practice

It is an old saying, and a true one, that everybody can warm up a champion but few can play with him. The implication is that during a practice session it's quite easy to slug the ball a lot—really hit it well—and delude yourself into thinking you're the greatest player in the history of the game, but when somebody says "play ball" your nerves tighten up or something else goes wrong and you slowly sink back to your own level. It's true. Practice is usually more relaxed than actual match play. You're loosened up, your mind is at ease, everything is copacetic—and before you know it you've turned what should be a very serious part of your tennis life into a lighthearted social happening.

Just as there is a correct way to approach tennis during match play, so is there a correct way to approach a practice session, and the first rule, about which there is no equivocating, is simply to work hard. Every rally during practice should be continued with all the determination and concentration you put into an actual point. Once you're sufficiently warmed up and have gotten the kinks out of your muscles, you should work full time toward getting into position before every shot, hitting every ball on the first bounce, and attempting to place every ground stroke, volley, service, and overhead exactly where you would want to during an actual match. Timing is of the essence, and at the highest level of the game, when the mechanical aspects of any shot are pretty much automatic, timing is not just of the essence, it is *everything*. And believe me, there is a great deal of difference, for example, between hitting a ball on the first bounce and hitting it on the second or even the third, which is what many players tend to do during practice. The spin is different, the pace is different, and even your attitude is different. If you are lazy in practice and do things in a slovenly manner, enjoyable as it may be, you are only acquiring poor habits, which will become harder and harder to break once you step on the court for real.

One thing you should do in practice is to hit the ball

harder than you would normally during a match. I have said it before, but the harder you hit the ball, the more you can attack and the better off you'll be. If you normally hit a slow-paced ball, hit a medium-paced one in practice. If you normally hit with medium pace, during practice clobber the devil out of the ball, but not at the expense of rhythm. Pretty soon you'll be hitting the ball as hard in a match as you do in practice, and that's perfect. You should also play by the book. During a match you obviously will hit the shot you feel safest with in a certain situation, whether it's the correct shot or not. In practice, you should always hit the correct shot. For example, if your forehand approach shot down the line isn't the best in the world, you're probably going to hit a lot of crosscourts during a match, which is wrong. So during practice, hit everything down the line. This is the only way to build confidence in your marginal shots, and if you work on them hard enough, you should be able to get them up to a good, usable level.

Using a backboard has both advantages and disadvantages, but, on balance, I think they're good things. You hit more balls against a backboard in fifteen minutes than you do in an entire set of actual play, and it does provide an opportunity to really groove your ground strokes. The problem is that every shot you hit against a backboard comes back in pretty much the same way, and if you're not careful you can hit a hundred forehands in a row and think you've got the greatest forehand going, when in fact in competition you'll be lucky if your opponent hits *two* shots in a row the same way. So, a backboard is better than not playing at all, but don't consider it a substitute for play with a real opponent.

There are a variety of drills that you can use both to make the practice time go faster and to improve certain weaknesses in your game. They give you particular things to concentrate on, and at the same time they're pretty good conditioners.

• In the first drill you hit nothing but forehands down the line; your practice partner on the other side of the net hits nothing but backhands down the line. This kind of drill is intended primarily to improve accuracy. You should aim for a target area no more than three feet in from the sideline and three feet in from the base line. After each shot, return to your normal position in the center of the court. This is important. Part of every ground stroke is the footwork involved in getting to the ball and then returning to the center of the court after you have hit it, and much of the effectiveness of this drill is diminished if you stand still between shots. After about ten minutes of this, switch to the other sideline so that you hit backhands down the line and your partner hits forehands.

• Now both you and your partner hit nothing but crosscourts, first forehands, then backhands. The same rules apply: aim for a small target area and make sure you get back to the center of the court after each shot.

• Next hit nothing but down-the-line shots, while your partner hits nothing but crosscourts. This means that you hit a forehand down the line, and your partner follows with a backhand crosscourt; you then hit a backhand down the line, and your partner hits a forehand crosscourt. This drill and its opposite—in which you hit crosscourt and your partner hits down the line —are especially good, not only for improving your accuracy, but for increasing your wind and general stamina. If you're not in good shape, you'll know it after about ten minutes of hitting this way.

• If you have trouble hitting the ball with proper depth, you and your partner should stand about three feet behind the base line and hit the ball as hard and as deep as you can. And by "deep" I mean behind the opposite base line. Aim for each other's feet. Hitting hard like this for five minutes or so is not only exhilarating and a great confidence builder, but you'll be surprised how few times you actually can hit the ball beyond the far base line. Only a handful of players hit their ground strokes with the proper depth. This will help you find the range.

• To improve your reflexes and your timing at the net, both you and your partner stand inside the service line and hit volleys at each other. Don't try to put the ball away, but aim for each other's stomach. There's nothing like a tennis ball coming hard at you from close range to improve lazy reflexes.

• A variation of this drill is for you to stand in the forehand service court and your partner to stand in his forehand service court, hitting crosscourt volleys at each other. Then switch and hit backhand crosscourt volleys. These are especially good drills for doubles, where the server's first volley is almost always hit in a crosscourt direction.

• The half-court drill places you at the net and your practice partner in the backcourt. The backcourt player attempts to get the ball past you any way he can and also attempts to make you run up and back by alternating lobs with short, slow returns. But both of you must keep the ball on only one half of the court. Again, this allows you both to hit a lot of shots in a short period of time, and it is a superb conditioner. After five minutes or so, switch places, and let your partner play from the net.

• The two-on-one drill is just what it sounds like— two players on one side of the net against you on the other. Your two opponents attempt to run you as much as they can, both from side to side and up and back, but at the same time they never go for winners, trying instead just to keep the ball in play. For your part, hit every shot on the first bounce, no matter how far or hard you have to run, and try for winners whenever you can. After a few minutes, go through the same thing, this time playing from the net. This is by far the most demanding of all the drills.

• To practice your service, there's nothing better than a bucket of balls. Put a handkerchief or a piece of cardboard down in a particular corner of the service court and then aim for it. This gets to be slightly tedious after a while, but it's the best way I can recommend for quickly getting in a lot of work on what is hopefully your most effective shot. If you've got somebody else to work with, let him practice his return of service at the same time, and then switch. The service return is one of the most important shots you have, and its practice should not be neglected.

However much you work on particular drills, or just "hit" the ball, remember that there is no substitute for actually playing. A typical practice session of, say, ninety minutes might include a half hour's work on three or four of the drills I have listed, depending on your particular strengths and weaknesses, but the rest of the time should be spent playing actual points, games, and sets. Play hard, but work especially on those parts of your game that need work. That, after all, is what practice is for.

Conditioning

The further you progress in your tennis career, the more important strength and stamina will become to your success; you simply must have the physical ability to go all out from the first point of a match to the last regardless of how long the match drags on or how appalling the heat and humidity might be. Long practice sessions are fine, and the drills I just mentioned will do a lot to keep you in reasonably good shape, but you have to do more than just hit a lot of tennis balls to keep in top condition.

This is where physical training comes in. Every sport

makes different demands on the body: an athlete who is in shape for swimming probably wouldn't last very long on a football field; likewise a well-conditioned basketball player would likely collapse if he were asked to run the mile. A tennis player must be able to move fluidly and rhythmically and to stop quickly and start up again in any direction. For this he needs strong, well-developed legs. For a powerful serve and overhead he must have a solid stomach and a strong back.

For women, there is one further and more basic consideration. Young girls usually don't grow up handling a football or a baseball, and when they start to play tennis they simply don't know how to throw properly. The unfamiliarity of this motion is akin to that of a right-hander trying to throw lefty. Since the correct service motion is especially like that of a baseball pitcher or a football quarterback, a girl should spend a lot of time learning how to throw things properly, with her right elbow high in the air and her left foot forward. A simple enough exercise, but one that is usually overlooked.

For men and women both, the suggestions and drills listed below are designed especially to increase the physical capacity of a tennis player so that he or she will be able to play the third (or fifth) set of a match with as much drive and determination as the first.

• To increase your endurance, there's nothing better than just plain running. Men should start at a half-mile and slowly work themselves up to where they can jog easily for at least three miles; women should eventually be able to jog for at least two miles without being unduly winded.

• To increase your capacity for quick stops and starts without getting tired, run hard for twenty yards, walk or jog for ten yards, and repeat. Your goal should be at least twenty-five repetitions.

• A variation of this is to run in place for ten seconds, rest for ten seconds, and repeat. Your goal: ten repetitions.

• To improve your footwork, quickly sidestep the width of the court with a racket in your hand and when you reach either sideline, swing at an imaginary ball. Shuffle as you move—don't cross your feet—and work up to a maximum of ten minutes.

• Similarly, run forward to the net as hard as you can, again with your racket in your hand, then run backward to the base line. Ten minutes.

• While you run in place, have someone hold a tennis ball in front of you and move it quickly to the right and left, up and back. As he does so, you take four or five quick steps following the direction of the ball. This jitterbug drill is a superb way to improve your reaction time, and if you can hold out for sixty seconds you're doing fine.

• Skip rope; not lazily, but as quickly as you can, first on one foot, then on the other, both forward and backward. Five minutes.

• The kangaroo hop is a killer, but an absolutely fantastic way to flatten your stomach muscles. From a standing position, jump straight up in the air as high as you can and, while keeping your back straight, clasp your knees to your chest with your arms. If you can work up to fifty of these quickly and without stopping (thirty for women), consider yourself in superb shape.

• A masochistic variation of the kangaroo hop is to jump straight up in the air and at the same time spread your legs and touch your toes with your hands. Only twenty-five repeats on this one.

Most of these drills are designed specifically for tennis and emphasize the development of those parts of the body which are most important to a tennis player. Everyone's body is different—likewise their physical capacity—and you'll have to decide for yourself where, or if, you need special work in other areas. Obviously, don't try to run through all of these drills the first day, but slowly build up to the point where you can do most of them comfortably. And finally, don't work on physical conditioning before you practice. The drills are fine after you have played, or, if the weather's bad, instead of playing. If you work out hard before practice, you won't be in any kind of shape to concentrate on playing the game, which is the most important thing of all.

Court Surfaces: Grass, Clay, and Cement

The tennis game we know is more properly called "lawn tennis." In its earliest days it was just that—a game played on somebody's front lawn—and because of tradition (rather too much tradition, in my opinion) there has been a great reluctance to do away with grass as the playing surface for many major championships. This is most unfortunate, because in the United States especially there are only a few good grass courts, and even the best are susceptible to blight, angry feet, and the whims of weather, all of which can rapidly create gaping holes in what is supposed to be a smooth, level surface. Nevertheless, it is important to know the characteristics of grass courts because if your game improves sufficiently you'll probably have to play on them some time or another.

A grass court is fast, faster than any other playing surface except wood. The bounce of the ball is invariably low, and, depending on the texture of the court, bad bounces can unfortunately be quite frequent. For these reasons it is imperative to avoid the backcourt and spend as much time as possible at the net. Pace is more effective the closer you are to the net, and if you take the ball in the air you obviously don't have to worry about bad bounces or hitting ground strokes off your shoetops. Also, because of the fastness of the court, sharply angled shots are much more effective on grass than they are on slower surfaces.

Because the court is soft and gives a lot under foot, grass is difficult to run on. And the problem is compounded if the grass is at all moist, because then the surface becomes downright slick. In this case you should run slightly flatfooted. You're going to need every bit of traction you can find to run to the ball, and especially to change directions. Players experiencing grass for the first time sometimes acquire "grass court knees" because they fall down a lot before they learn to come to a complete stop and balance themselves perfectly before they change direction and start out after a ball.

A clay court has nearly all of the opposite characteristics of a grass court. The bounce of the ball is generally uniform, rather high, and the pace is quite slow. For these reasons, a ball that is an easy winner on grass or other fast surfaces may be nothing more than just another shot on clay. Therefore, even if you play the big serve-and-volley game, you should plan on hitting at least one more shot per point. The biggest problem a grass-court player has when he switches to clay is being patient. It's terribly frustrating to be passed just after you think you've hit a winning volley, and often a good clay court player will drive a good grass-court player to distraction simply by playing the waiting game—by not rushing his shots and at the same time waiting for his opponent to make an error.

Don't come to the net on clay unless you have hit a near-perfect approach shot. Be content to stay in the backcourt and move your opponent around until you are positive that your approach shots will be effective.

Also, learn to slide on clay. The best clay court players will slide as much as six feet into a shot. This is less tiring than taking that extra step or two to get to the ball, it will improve your timing, and it will make it easier for you to change direction and get into position for the next shot.

Cement, my own preference, is about halfway between grass and clay in terms of how it affects the speed of the ball and its bounce. Depending on the topping, of which there are many kinds, a cement (or other hard-composition) court can be lightning fast or deceptively slow, and the only general comment that can be made is that you can't slide very well on any of them. Don't try; you'll break an ankle.

Wind, Sun, and Heat

Playing tennis on a windy day is about the most miserable thing I can think of. A proper tennis court is surrounded by windbreaks made of canvas or plastic and these do afford some protection. But even in a place like the stadium at Forest Hills, where the courts are surrounded by a concrete bowl, there often is plenty of swirling wind down on the courts. When the wind is bad, the first thing to do is take comfort in the knowledge that your opponent is more or less going through the same anguish you are. The second is to make the wind work to your advantage. A tennis ball weighs only about two ounces, and if, for example, you hit into the wind it's going to drop to the ground a lot more quickly than if the wind is at your back. So on one side of the court don't hesitate to hit the ball a little harder than you might normally, and conversely, when you hit with the wind concentrate more on aiming your shots and less on slugging the ball.

A good antidote for wind is spin. Whether it's underspin or topspin really doesn't matter; the important thing is not to hit the ball perfectly flat, even if that is normally your preference. On a windy day a ball hit without any spin will wobble all over the place, and you won't have any idea where it's going. Spin will give you at least some degree of control.

One particular shot—the lob—deserves special consideration. Avoid lobbing with the wind unless you're pretty sure you've got a winner. Unless you have perfect touch, once that little fuzzy ball gets up into the atmosphere, it's gone forever. On the other hand, lob often into the wind, especially if you are on the defensive. You can get away with murder, because a strong breeze will hold almost every lob you hit in the court.

The second biggest problem is the sun. Most tennis courts are laid out north to south so that neither player must stare directly into the sun, but on occasion you're going to go back to serve, toss the ball up—and find yourself blinded. There are only two things you can do, besides hoping for a cloud. Either take a couple of steps to the left or right, or toss the ball up a foot or so away from the spot where you normally would. Neither of these remedies is going to help your service very much, but you've got to see the ball before you can hit it, and that should be your prime consideration.

Also, rely more on your lob when your opponent is facing the sun. Many times he will be forced to let the ball drop, but even if he isn't, hitting a well-placed lob with the sun in his eyes won't be very pleasant.

On an insufferably hot or humid day, keep just one thing in mind, and that is to make sure your opponent does more running than he has ever done in his life. Hit a lot of drop shots and lobs, or hit from side to side—anything that forces him to expend a lot of energy. Even if the results aren't immediately apparent, by the end of the second set or midway through the third he is going to start feeling the strain. At the same time, you should make sure that you yourself don't waste a lot of energy unnecessarily. If you find yourself getting tired, just slow down the pace of the match a little.

Court Conduct

Finally, let me offer a few guidelines for court conduct. There is sometimes a fine line between what you can legitimately do on a tennis court and what constitutes unethical gamesmanship, or worse. But if you follow these suggestions, which really boil down to questions of good manners, you will help yourself become not only a better tennis player, but a good sportsman as well.

1. Never lose your temper. At best this can sometimes turn into an expensive habit; rackets don't bounce very well. At worst, it can cause you to get so worked up that there is no way for you to play good tennis. Keep on an even keel before, during, and after a match. If you show your emotions too much you are only giving your opponent another bit of information that he might be able to use against you. Sometimes it helps to get angry at yourself, and within bounds there's nothing at all wrong with this. It can help you bear down on the job at hand. But don't let your opponent know you're working yourself up. It will only make him concentrate more himself.

2. Play to win all the time. There is nothing more disgusting than to see a player who is trailing badly in

a match stop trying completely. And equally distasteful is the player who is winning easily and rubs in his superiority by cutting up or fooling around against his hapless opponent. Either way, it's bad manners. If you're losing and give up, you detract from your opponent's victory; if you're winning and start playing around, you only embarrass your opponent.

3. Be gracious in both victory and defeat. Being a good winner is occasionally difficult, but if you flaunt your victory, the next time you meet that particular player you may have a tiger on your hands. In defeat, congratulate your opponent on a match well played and then, if you must, get mad as heck at yourself. But do it in private. After all, you can't bring the match back (although you can learn from it), and making a scene in public will only alienate you from everyone you know.

4. Don't stall on the court and, on the other hand, don't attempt to rush things by quick-serving or otherwise hurrying your opponent. All are patently unethical and quick-serving is downright illegal. However, don't hesitate to try to establish a match tempo that is to your own liking—and possibly to your opponent's disliking. If he plays very quickly and doesn't take much time between points or games, slow things down a little bit. This is perfectly legal; you're allowed a reasonable amount of time to set yourself between points and at the change. At the same time, if your opponent tends to be slow, play the points as quickly as you can—or want to.

5. Know the rules of lawn tennis. Not just the obvious ones, but the weird ones as well. You may be confronted with a strange situation—like a ball breaking or a net falling down—once in a lifetime, but you should know the proper rulings, both for your own benefit and to avoid arguments.

6. If there is no umpire or linesman for your match, make your calls quickly and clearly, and if you're not sure whether a ball is in or out, give your opponent a reasonable benefit of the doubt.

10 | Notes from Center Court

As I mentioned back in the first chapter, practically from the first day I stepped onto a tennis court I preferred playing up at the net to standing around in the backcourt. I liked it up there and just sort of automatically went forward whenever I could get away with it. My coach was right, of course, in insisting that I first learn a good forehand and backhand, because trying to volley before you know how to hit ground strokes is sort of like a pianist trying to play "The Flight of the Bumblebee" before he knows his scales. I didn't know what I was doing; I was just learning the game. But I suppose it was a matter of personality. I wanted to hit the ball before it bounced because I liked the quickness of it. Just hit the serve and go to the net. If I made it I made it; if I missed it I missed it. And, making allowances for a few years' experience, that's how I play now.

I mention this story to emphasize again that tennis is an individual game. Certain techniques and certain strategies are pretty basic, but beyond the fundamentals no two players really approach the game the same way. And thank goodness for that. For players and spectators alike, tennis would be utterly boring if everybody did exactly the same things in exactly the same way. If you like to hit the ball hard and with a lot of flair, then by all means do so (besides, that's what I recommend anyhow); but if you like to stand in the backcourt and play a nice, steady game, then by all means do that. You should tailor your game to your personality. Don't try to change your personality to accommodate your tennis game. It just won't fit.

To my way of thinking, there are two ways to approach tennis. The first is as a means of pleasant exercise which you and your whole family or group of friends can enjoy—the sport for a lifetime. An hour's tennis two or three times a week at the park or the club is a convenient and enjoyable way to stay in shape, to make friends (and maybe an enemy or two), and to keep generally in good physical and mental health. This is certainly a perfectly good goal. Nine million or so Americans play tennis, but only a few thousand are serious tournament competitors and only a couple of hundred, if that many, play in world-class competition on the international circuit. For the rest, tennis is an enjoyable therapy, a time out from the rigors of running a household, studying for exams, or whatever. If you are learning the game just for fun, so be it.

But for those of you who aspire to play something more than social tennis, let me suggest a few things. I don't mean to give the impression that once you decide to set a competitive goal for yourself—whether it's to play at Wimbledon or merely to move up from number five to number four on the school tennis team —all the fun is suddenly going to disappear from the game. Quite the contrary, except that now your enjoyment, instead of coming from the social relaxation tennis provides, will come, hopefully, from the sense that you are moving toward the mastery of an extremely complex and difficult game. I emphasize "moving toward" because there is no such thing as the perfect tennis player any more than there is the perfect writer, perfect politician, or perfect anything else. Even at the sport's highest level many more points are lost through errors than won through placements, and as long as the human factor is present, perfectibility is out of the question. The enjoyment I get from tennis comes from the knowledge that there is always something new to learn or improve upon. When I was a teen-ager I once went through a period when I lost at least ten matches because I couldn't hit one shot—a forehand down the line. Just that one shot. Finally I realized that if I was going to get anywhere I had to learn to hit a forehand down the line. So I worked at it, got that shot down, and then moved on to something else.

Then, too, I enjoy winning matches. I don't like it a bit if I spend three hours under the hot sun and come off the court a loser. It just isn't quite as much fun. And this may be an obvious point, but you have got to *want* to be the best before you can even begin to reach for that goal, and you have got to be prepared to sacrifice a lot to get there. Here's a typical situation: You go up to a junior player, and a good one, too—maybe he's been around the world a couple of times and has a pretty high ranking—and you ask him, "Do you want to win Wimbledon? Really?" And he'll give you a look like you're crazy or something and say,

"Sure. Doesn't everybody?" But then you keep talking to him and pretty soon you find out that he doesn't really know what it's all about. It's easy enough to say you want to win, but you really have to feel it deep down inside, too. I know I didn't feel it that way until 1964, the year I quit college and left behind my fiancé (we were later married, so that worked out all right) and went to Australia to take lessons from Mervyn Rose. In college I had hardly touched my racket from each September until the following May. There's no way to become number one if you do things like that. The layoff had been a nice excuse for my failures— you can always find an excuse if you want to—but that's about all.

You have got to want to win, but as a beginner you've got to think about other things too. I began playing in tournaments six months after I first picked up a racket. I was always erratic and I lost to everybody. I spent the time clobbering the hide off the ball and lost to all sorts of pushers who would just stand on the base line and keep hitting the ball back nice and easy and wait for me to make errors. Which I did. But my coach always told me not to worry about winning or losing, but to learn an all-round game no matter what, because in the long run it would pay off. If you play an aggressive game when you start out you may lose to these pushers, too. But I promise you, if you develop a good forehand, a good backhand, and a good serve, volley and overhead—a solid all-round game without any glaring weaknesses—you'll make it. It takes a certain kind of person to accept this sort of thing. Most people want immediate results. They would rather win right away—be good in the fourteen-and-unders and sixteen-and-unders—and have a lot of those pretty trophies up on the shelf. But you just can't worry about that. You may lose now, but if you stick with it you'll one day start beating those pushers, and then the matches will be a lot more important than they are right now.

The problem I had with my forehand down the line relates to this, too. The reason I couldn't hit one was simple—I didn't work on it. I goofed around and got away with murder because I could always get to the net pretty well, and if you're at the net you don't have to worry about hitting a forehand down the line, or anywhere else. And if I did have to hit a forehand, I could always be real clever and fake a shot down the line and then flick it crosscourt. Pretty soon, though, the good players got onto that. They knew I couldn't hit down the line and so they didn't worry about covering that side of their court at all, and I suddenly found myself in all sorts of trouble, trouble I could have avoided if I had learned the shot right at the beginning.

You have got to think on a tennis court. It is true that at the highest level of the game the players move to the ball and hit a particular shot pretty much by instinct. By that I mean that when I prepare to hit a shot now, I don't think of the specific way I'm going to grip my racket or consciously decide, say, to hit a backhand down the line or crosscourt, or with a lot of topspin or flat. By now that sort of thing comes naturally. It's just like typing. A good typist doesn't consciously think about what finger she's going to hit a certain key with, she just types. But just as it takes time for a typist to reach that level, so does it take a tennis player time—

a long time—to reach the point where the basic strategies of percentage tennis are more or less automatic.

To learn the whys of tennis you have to be a keen student of the game. When I was younger I never enjoyed watching tennis, except perhaps when two of the very best players were on the court. I preferred to play. But when I was in Australia Merv Rose made me sit down and watch matches all day long—that is, when I wasn't playing myself. He would sit next to me and make me try to figure out certain things: like why players hit first services where they do, what kind of approach shots work best and why others don't work so well, and so on. I had to become aware of *why* players hit certain shots in particular situations, and this not only helped me to learn about my potential opponents, it helped me to understand my own game, too.

This is the sort of thing that can really make a difference, but you'd be surprised at the number of top juniors who, when they walk off the court, can't begin to tell you why they won or lost a particular match, or which shots worked for them and which didn't. For example, a player may spend an entire afternoon and not hit one successful passing shot, and afterward if you ask him why he didn't lob more or try hitting right at his opponent, he'll just shrug his shoulders. This is sad as well as stupid.

At the end of every match you should be able to remember everything that worked for you as well as everything that maybe didn't work so well, and at the same time, which shots of your opponent's were effective and which weren't. This is elementary. If you need to, compile a card catalog on both your game and those of your opponents. It's a simple enough thing to do, and can come in handy the next time you play somebody who gives you a hard time.

Keep your emotions under control. Not just your temper, which should always be held in check anyway, but anything at all that might give away how you feel on a particular day. Sometimes you're just not going to want to play tennis, and the chances are you won't play very well either. Even the best players have days when absolutely nothing seems to go right—on the court and off—and the better player you become, the worse your bad days will be. And it's a funny thing. If you're feeling marvelous and playing great, winning doesn't mean too much. But if you have to fight and really scratch and claw to get out of a match—and can do it—then somehow that means more than just a routine victory.

Keeping cool doesn't mean, though, that you shouldn't try and key yourself up before a match. Some players are so nervous when they step on the court they can't hit a ball straight for five or ten minutes. Others can't seem to get worked up until they've fallen way behind and are in real danger of losing. I personally don't like to think about a match at all until about ten minutes before I walk onto the court. Then I like to be off by myself. No one bugging me. Just me by myself. And what I think about is how much it's going to hurt me if I lose. Sometimes it's easy to forget how you feel when you lose, but as soon as I start thinking about a couple of matches that I've lost in the past, I get a really weird feeling. Losing takes something out of you—or at least it should—almost as if there's a certain void that you can never fill because you can never bring that match back. I lost in the finals of Wimbledon in 1963 and I still get sick thinking about that match, even when I'm not about to walk onto the court.

Beyond natural ability, I look for three things in a player just starting out. Does he hate to lose? Does he think about tennis, and in particular about the matches he plays himself? And does he work hard at his game?

Ask yourself these questions. If you can honestly answer yes to every one, you might play on Center Court yourself someday. I hope you make it.

Index